$3.50

# THE TRIUMPH OF MAXIMILIAN I

*137 Woodcuts by Hans Burgkmair and Others*

*With a translation of descriptive text,
introduction and notes by
Stanley Appelbaum*

# THE TRIUMPH OF MAXIMILIAN I:

*137 Woodcuts by Hans Burgkmair and Others*

*With a translation of descriptive text, introduction and notes by* STANLEY APPELBAUM

DOVER PUBLICATIONS, INC.   NEW YORK

Published in the United Kingdom by Constable and Company, Limited, 10 Orange Street, London W.C.2.

The plates in the present edition of *The Triumph of Maximilian I* are reproduced from the one edited by Franz Schestag and published by Adolf Holzhausen in Vienna in 1883–84 for the *Jahrbuch* of the Kunsthistorische Sammlungen des Allerhöchsten Kaiserhauses.

The present edition also contains a new Introduction and Bibliography, and a new, annotated translation of the Descriptive Text (based on the texts in the Bartsch edition of 1796 and the Holzhausen edition of 1883–84), especially prepared for this Dover edition by Stanley Appelbaum.

*International Standard Book Number: 0-486-21207-6*
*Library of Congress Catalog Card Number: 63-19488*

Manufactured in the United States of America

Dover Publications, Inc.
180 Varick Street
New York 14, N. Y.

# *Contents*

THE PLATES

GENERAL VIEW OF THE '*TRIUMPH*'

# *Introduction*

In its boldness of conception, its epic proportions, and its wealth of content, the *Triumph of Maximilian I* stands as one of the world's richest and most unusual monuments of art. It is a sequence of 137 woodcuts by the foremost graphic artists in the German realms, created at the moment when wood engraving had reached its fullest flowering. In one splendid sheet after another it portrays the achievements and aspirations, the dreams of eternity and the earthly pleasures, of the most colorful and paradoxical ruler of his time.

Admired by some historians for his revivification of the Holy Roman Empire and his preparation for future territorial expansion, reviled by as many others for his neglect of the Empire's internal problems and his depletion of the treasury in long and needless wars, the Emperor Maximilian enjoys the perennial esteem of the whole civilized world for his passionate dedication to the arts, sciences, and intellectual currents of his day. Yet despite his countless commissions for histories, musical dramas, sculptures, architectural projects, paintings, and other works of art, his name is particularly associated with the woodcut; indeed, at least one thousand woodcuts were executed in his service.

Fond as he was of entertainments and traditions that harked back to medieval times, still this "last of the knights" (born 1459, died 1519) possessed a sense of the power of publicity unique in his day. He saw clearly how he could enhance the glory of himself and his Hapsburg dynasty through the widest possible dissemination of inspiring words and pictures. The woodcut was the ideal medium for his purpose. From its obscure beginnings in southern Germany about 1400 as a cheap technique for reproducing art and lettering, the woodcut had risen by the end of the fifteenth century to unheard-of brilliance as a medium of illustration in books and in separate sheets. Maximilian was fortunate enough to be living and reigning when men like Albrecht Dürer of Nuremberg and Hans Burgkmair of Augsburg had brought the art of the woodcut to heights that have never been surpassed.

The Emperor made no secret of his purpose in commissioning these expensive works even though his treasury was chronically empty:

> Whoever prepares no memorial for himself during his lifetime has none after his death and is forgotten along with the sound of the bell that tolls his passing. Thus the money I spend for the perpetuation of my memory is not lost; in fact, in such a matter to be sparing of money is to suppress my future memory.

Of the many woodcut works executed for Maximilian, three books and two cycles are outstanding. The *Weisskunig* is an allegorical autobiography of the Emperor (written with the aid of his secretaries) in which he appears as the "White King," and other real persons and nations are cloaked in a simple color symbolism. Burgkmair contributed 117 of the 251 woodcut illustrations, and some critics consider these to be his best work.

The *Theuerdank* (that is, "The Knight of Adventurous Thoughts," also Maximilian in a thin disguise) is a long poem about the Emperor's youth and his stirring courtship of Mary of Burgundy, the beloved wife he lost after a brief five years of marriage. Most of the 118 woodcuts were by Hans Schäufelein; 14 were by Burgkmair.

The *Freydal* is an account of the tournaments and masquerades in which Maximilian participated during his happy days in Burgundy. The woodcuts were by various artists, five by Dürer. Of these three books only the *Theuerdank* was ready for publication in Maximilian's lifetime. It appeared in 1517, and was the most sumptuous book of its era.

The Emperor also saw the completion of one of the two great woodcut cycles that he planned in the last decade of his life—the *Ehrenpforte* (*Triumphal Arch*). The *Arch*, first printed in 1517, is a vast two-dimensional edifice over ten feet high, composed of 92 separate sheets. Dürer was general artistic director and author of some of the sheets; his pupil Hans Springinklee provided many others. Pictures of Maximilian's ancestors, his wars, and key moments of his political life are framed in a rich setting of fanciful architecture.

But for the culmination of his artistic enterprises, for what would be his last look backward at a restless and eventful life, Maximilian chose the timeless symbolism of the triumphal procession. The practice of a grand entry into a city by a victorious ruler or conqueror had lingered on in Christianized form throughout the Middle Ages, but the Renaissance awakening of passionate interest in the details of ancient Roman forms and ceremonies, as well as the incredible popularity of Petrarch's *Trionfi*, had made the trappings of the triumph a frequent feature in works of art, particularly in Italy. In 1492, the year before Maximilian put on the crown of the Holy Roman Empire, Andrea Mantegna completed his Mantuan cycle of nine large paintings known as the *Triumph of Caesar*, now in Hampton Court. This was the most ambitious and most admired conception of the triumph up to that time: it included brass players, soldiers holding painted battle scenes, trophy-bearers, elephants, noble prisoners, banners, and Caesar on his triumphal car—all elements that we come upon again in Maximilian's *Triumph*.

But the similarities (and it is almost certain that Maximilian or his artists knew Mantegna's work) only lead us to admire the more the originality, the intensity of personal flavor, the uniqueness of the Hapsburg *Triumph*. The people who parade before us here are real people, the Emperor's courtiers and servants, dressed not in togas but in rich contemporary costume. Maximilian's *Triumph* celebrates his own pleasures—hunts, tournaments, music; his own inventions in artillery and siegecraft; the fruition of his most cherished political and dynastic schemes; the soldiery that he created; his loyal knights. Although this *Triumph* is the result of the planning and labors of numerous counselors, historians, painters, graphic artists, and wood engravers, the viewer feels on every sheet the presence and the guiding hand of the Emperor. And, indeed, it is in Maximilian's words that we read the full description of the *Triumph*.

In 1512 Maximilian dictated to his secretary Marx Treitzsaurwein the plan for the painted version of the *Triumph*—the rich paintings on vellum in miniature technique were to be the Emperor's personal treasure, while the woodcut version would belong to the world. Jörg Kölderer, architect and designer, prepared the sketches that served both the painters and the woodcut designers. In Kölderer's studio, perhaps with the participation of Albrecht Altdorfer and Wolf Huber, the 109 miniatures were executed (numbers 1–49 exist today only in copies). The commissions for the woodcut designs were given to artists in Nuremberg and Augsburg.

The leading painter and draughtsman in the wealthy city of Augsburg (important as a center of trade with Italy and as the home of the Fuggers) was Hans Burgkmair (1473–1531). Of all of Maximilian's major artists, Burgkmair was the one who adapted his talents most fully and wholeheartedly to the service of the Emperor. Burgkmair had studied painting with his father Thoman, other Augsburg masters, and possibly with Martin Schongauer in Colmar. He almost certainly had visited Venice and northern Italy (before 1500), for no other German painter of his generation absorbed more of the Venetian feeling for color and the modeling of the human form. His painted *œuvre* includes many fine religious and historical works and portraits. But he is best remembered for his graphic productions—Bible illustrations; series of virtues, planets, and worthy Jews, Christians, and pagans; many book illustrations for the Augsburg printer Stainer; coats of arms; ornaments; and much more. He experimented brilliantly with colored and chiaroscuro woodcut techniques. A critic of the stature of William Ivins, late Curator of Prints at the Metropolitan Museum of Art, has claimed that while Burgkmair may fall short of Dürer as a powerful universal artist, he may possibly surpass the Nuremberg master in the perfect appropriateness of his woodcut drawings to the exigencies of the technique and his full appreciation of the problems of the wood engraver (rarely in those days the same man who drew the design on the block). Burgkmair drew 66 of the 137 woodcuts of the *Triumph*, numbers 1–56, 111–114, 123–125, and 129–131. Other woodcuts by this artist, of great significance for the background of the present work, are discussed in the notes to the descriptive text of the *Triumph*.

Albrecht Altdorfer, Hans Springinklee, Leonhard Beck, Hans Schäufelein, and Wolf Huber have been credited with other sections of the work; specific attributions are discussed in the notes. Dürer, who seems to have felt little personal enthusiasm for the project, is responsible for only sheets 89 and 90, and a few sheets that do not form part of the *Triumph* itself.

As the woodcut designs (which are far from being slavish imitations of the sketches and paintings) were completed, they were cut by seventeen different engravers (or twelve, according to how the names on the backs of the blocks are read). The project came to an end, however, after Maximilian died on January 12, 1519. A comparison of the text and paintings with the woodcut work shows how much more was still to be done; but in its incomplete form, the *Triumph* still radiates an impression of grandeur, breadth, and sweep that are almost unparalleled in the history of art.

The first edition of the *Triumph* appeared in 1526; impressions from this edition are now of the greatest rarity. Afterwards the original blocks were kept partly at Ambras in the Tyrol and partly at Graz in Styria. Two blocks (numbers 90 and 132 in the present book) were lost before 1777, when impressions were pulled at Ambras and Graz from the blocks in those two collections (together, these impressions count officially as the second edition).

In 1779 all the blocks in existence were reunited in Vienna, where the important third edition was published in book form in 1796; the scholar Adam Bartsch was responsible for this edition, although his name does not appear in the book. The 1796 edition, like that of 1777, contains only 135 woodcuts.

The Holbein Society in England was the next publisher to present the *Triumph* in its complete form, although reduced in size. But the Society's publication of 1873–75 does not count officially as an "edition," because it was reproduced not from the original blocks, but from early impressions. This version was thus able to include the two sheets for which the blocks had been lost, but the quality of reproduction throughout is not especially good.

The fourth and last edition was printed and published by Adolf Holzhausen in Vienna in 1883–84 for the *Jahrbuch* of the Vienna Kunsthistorisches Museum (then the "Kunsthistorische Sammlungen des Allerhöchsten Kaiserhauses"); Franz Schestag was the editor. For this edition impressions newly pulled from the original blocks were photomechanically reproduced in facsimile; numbers 90 and 132 were, naturally, reproductions of earlier impressions. Ivins considered the Holzhausen edition the finest and most faithful since the first edition of 1526. It is this 1883–84 edition—now itself extremely costly and found only in large libraries and collections—that is the basis of the present volume.

It is impossible to overestimate the importance of the *Triumph* as a primary source for the history of costume, musical instruments, heraldry, and military and sporting weapons, armor, and appurtenances; for portraits of individual historical characters; and for hundreds of authentic and unusual ornamental motifs. We hope that the volume we now offer to the public will win for the *Triumph* the wider recognition and popularity it so well deserves.

*New York*                                               STANLEY APPELBAUM
*1964*

## GENERAL NOTE ON THE PLATES

The plates of this Dover publication were reproduced from the 1883–84 Holzhausen edition at a uniform reduction of 47 percent. They are arranged on our pages in the sequence 2, 1; 4, 3; 6, 5, etc., in order to preserve the feeling of a procession moving toward the right. In addition, we have included at the end a novel feature: a highly reduced version of the complete *Triumph* on 10 pages, which allows an immediate survey of the scope, continuity, and inner coherence of the entire vast work of art.

## NOTE ON THE PRESENT TRANSLATION

The basic text here translated is that of a 1512 manuscript preserved in Vienna, which contains the plan for the miniature paintings of the *Triumph* (thus including many subjects which were never cut in wood). At the time Maximilian dictated this text to his secretary, most of the verse inscriptions had not yet been composed. All sections here enclosed within parentheses—verse inscriptions and a few other passages—are additions to this basic text taken from the miniature paintings themselves or from another manuscript of the period, written shortly after Maximilian's death. This will furnish the reader with the fullest possible contemporary description of the *Triumph* and with the complete text of the verses that were to have appeared on many of the woodcuts. Square brackets within the text indicate passages supplied by modern editors to describe woodcuts that were not covered in the sixteenth-century texts. The footnotes contain explanatory material compiled by the present translator.

Bartsch included in his 1796 edition of the *Triumph* a French translation of this descriptive text which, apart from a few errors and omissions, covered the prose sections quite well, but gave only the gist of the verse inscriptions in a few words of prose. The English version supplied by Alfred Aspland in the 1873–75 Holbein Society publication appears to be a rather slavish translation of the 1796 *French* text, but slightly abridged and with a few new errors. The present translation, based on the original German, is the first to reproduce the inscriptions fully and in the form of verse.

The numbers of the woodcuts are given to the left of their description. (The square braces accompanying these numbers distinguish those portions of the text that apply to the woodcuts; the rest of the text applies to those miniatures from which woodcuts were never produced.) The plate numbers referred to are always those established by Schestag for his 1883–84 edition; these are the large numbers that run throughout consecutively. Beginning with number 89, there are also small numbers printed beneath the Schestag numbers: these were the numbers used by Bartsch in his 1796 edition. Scholars still often refer to Bartsch's numbers rather than Schestag's. It will be noted that numbers 90 and 132 of the present edition are marked "Not in B[artsch]." The woodblocks for these two subjects were lost some time between the editions of 1526 and 1777. They were not included in Bartsch. Schestag reproduced them from impressions of the first (1526) edition.

S. A.

*The Triumph of Maximilian I*

# Triumph of the Emperor Maximilian, first of this name, of glorious memory

What is written in this book was personally dictated by Emperor Maximilian in the year 1512 to me, Marx Treitzsaurwein, his Imperial Majesty's secretary.

The following tells how Emperor Maximilian's triumph is to be made, arranged, and painted.

### HERALD (ANNOUNCER OF THE TRIUMPH)

1 At the beginning shall be a naked man riding on a griffin [1] (monster or chimera) without a saddle; this naked man shall have nothing else on, because the animal's wing shall cover his privy parts. In his hand he shall bear a strange twisted horn and shall be blowing it, and this naked man shall be called thus: herald (announcer of the triumph), and he shall be wearing a laurel wreath.

### TITLE

2 Then two horses shall bear a litter, and the horses shall be led by two grooms, and on the litter shall be a large plaque in Italian style, well ornamented, in which the following title is to be written: [2]

### TITLE OF THE EMPEROR'S TRIUMPH

2 To the most illustrious mighty prince and lord, Maximilian, Roman Emperor Elect and head of Christendom, also king and heir of seven Christian kingdoms, Archduke of Austria, Duke of Burgundy [3] and of other mighty principalities and territories in Europe, and so forth; in praise and eternal memory of his honorable pleasures, imperial nature, and warlike conquests, this Triumph with the decoration of its arrangement is dedicated.

### FIFERS AND DRUMMERS

3 Then shall be depicted Anthony the fifer (of Dornstätt) on horseback, carrying his verse inscription, and he shall be distinguished

---

[1] Fabulous and exotic animals, legacies of medieval allegorical bestiaries, were popular features in live as well as pictured triumphs. In Francis I's triumphal *entrée* into Caen in 1532, the Nine Worthies took part, with Joshua riding on an elephant, David on a camel, Judas Maccabeus on a stag, Hector on a unicorn, Alexander on a griffin, and Julius Caesar on a dromedary (the Christian Worthies rode horses). See also woodcuts 17, 19, 21, 23, and 25.

[2] When work on the woodblocks was abandoned after the death of Maximilian, the solid areas of these inscription plaques had not yet been carved away to let the shapes of the letters stand out, and all these areas printed solid black in the editions of 1526 and 1777. Bartsch had some of these plaque areas cut out completely for his 1796 edition, since he felt that the solid black was highly prejudicial to the appearance of the printed sheets; thus today there are some all-black and some all-white inscription areas. Aspland in his 1873–75 publication (not reproduced from the original blocks) had all these areas appear in white.

[3] Maximilian became Duke of Burgundy at the age of eighteen when he married Mary, heiress to this still independent buffer state between France and Germany. He made an adventurous ride across Europe to claim his betrothed when Louis XI of France coveted her hand and lands for his Dauphin.

in his dress from the other fifers; he shall carry his fife case and wear a long sword, and his verse shall read thus:

> I, Anthony of Dornstätt, have played my fife
> For Maximilian, great in strife,
> In many lands on countless journeys,
> In battles fierce and knightly tourneys,
> At grave times or in holiday,
> And so in this Triumph with honor I play.

3

> (Gladly and oft my fife I blew
> In proper style, with honor true,
> Serving the Imperial arms
> In knightly joust and war's alarms.
> Always prepared, the fifer blows
> Tunes gay and stern, as this Triumph shows.)

Behind him shall be three fifers abreast in good order on horseback (in traditional military jackets and blue caps with plumes) in the act of playing their fifes; they shall have their fife cases and long swords instead of rapiers.

4

Behind them shall be five drummers abreast in good order on horseback in the act of beating their drums (in traditional dress); they shall all have long swords.[4]

The fifers and drummers shall all wear laurel wreaths.

### Falconry [5]

5

Then shall come on horseback a falconer, distinguished from the other falconers in dress, who shall be the master falconer, Hans Teuschel by name; he shall have a falcon lure and shall be

---

[4] Preparatory pen drawings by Burgkmair for this woodcut and for number 9 have come down to us.

[5] Maximilian celebrated his hunts in the text and woodcuts of the *Weisskunig* and *Theuerdank* also. The Louvre possesses a tapestry sequence, executed in the 1530's, which is known as the *Hunts of Maximilian* and depicts some of the same clothing and equipment shown in the *Triumph* (later copies of the April and September tapestries of this sequence are in the Metropolitan Museum of Art). See also note 43.

---

dressed like a falconer; he shall bear a verse inscription, which shall read thus:

By order of his Imperial Majesty he improved falconry, so that it could be enjoyed both summer and winter.

5

> (The Emperor, planning constantly,
> Has raised the art of falconry,
> Making joys of summer and winter the same,
> And ordering me to make my aim
> The quest of pleasure of every sort
> At all times with this feathered sport.)

6

Following him shall come five falconers abreast in good order on horseback; four of them shall bear a falcon on their hand, and the fifth shall bear an owl;[6] the falconers shall have falcon lures and be dressed like falconers, and one of them shall bear a falcon perch. The falconers shall all have laurel wreaths.

In the air before the falconers three falcons shall be flying; one shall be catching a heron, the second a vulture, the third a duck.

### Ibex and Chamois Hunting

7

After them shall come a chamois hunter on horseback, dressed to suit his calling; this shall be Conrad Zuberle, who shall bear the following verse inscription:

> (After ibex and chamois he'd never quail
> The loftiest mountain crag to scale.
> I did promote this merry chase
> As was desired by His Grace
> And as he then commanded me—
> And many marveled, this sport to see!)

He painstakingly arranged it for the Emperor that there should be the merriest ibex and chamois hunting in the world.

After him shall come five animals, including both ibex and chamois.

---

[6] The owl was used to attract kites and similar birds into the range of the falcons.

After them shall come on foot five chamois hunters in hose and doublets with their high chamois shoes,[7] also with their crampons,[8] haversacks, socketed knives, snow rings,[9] and chamois spears, pointed beneath, with the socketed knives attached on top.

The chamois hunters shall all have laurel wreaths.

### DEER HUNTING

Conrad von Rot shall be chief deer hunter and, riding on horseback, shall carry his verse inscription; he shall be dressed (in a traditional jacket) more finely than the other deer hunters and shall also carry a curved Dutch hunting horn.   His verse shall be as follows:

That in accordance with the Emperor's instructions he frequently arranged merry deer hunts on mountains and plains, giving great pleasure.

> (To fell fine stags was all his care
> On hill and dale, with trap and snare
> Or overtaking them in chase
> In many a thickly wooded place.
> By his Imperial order guided,
> Much joyous sport I thus provided.)

After him shall come five deer abreast.

Then five deer hunters (in traditional jackets) shall come abreast in good order on horseback; they shall have hunting knives but no swords; in their hands they shall bear switches, and they too shall have curved Dutch horns.

The hunters shall all have laurel wreaths.

### BOAR HUNTING

Wilhelm von Greyssen shall be chief boar hunter and, riding on horseback, shall bear his verse; he shall be dressed as a boar hunter, but more finely than the others; his verse shall be as follows:

[7] These were tied above the ankle to keep out pebbles, etc.

[8] These were iron spikes tied beneath the shoes with leather bands, to prevent slipping on icy climbs.

[9] These are the large rings by their sides, a kind of snowshoe.

By order of the Emperor he arranged fierce boar hunts to the greatest satisfaction.

> (The boar hunt, too, so fierce and grim
> Was source of such delight to him,
> He raised it to this great degree,
> Planning for it constantly.
> And by his wish and designation
> I make this sport my occupation.)

After him shall come five boars painted as wild as possible.

Then shall follow five boar hunters on horseback with their new boar swords and spears, which they shall carry unsheathed.

They shall also bear German hunting horns.

And the boar hunters shall all be wearing laurel wreaths.

### BEAR HUNTING

After them shall come on horseback the chief bear hunter, Herr Diepolt von Slandersberg, wearing a fine bear hunter's costume, with a large hunting horn; he shall bear his verse, which shall read thus:

That by the Emperor's instructions he instituted a rare new style in fearsome bear hunting and occasioned great pleasure.

> (No effort did he ever spare
> In hunts for many a fearsome bear
> In old ways and in new style, too,
> And this achieved with honor true.
> To further this he ordered me,
> Respecting all rules of venery.)

After him shall follow five bears abreast; some of the bears shall look back fiercely at the bear hunters.

After them shall come on foot five bear hunters abreast, dressed in short jackets, tightly girt; they shall carry hunting knives and each shall have a bear spear.

The bear hunters shall all be wearing laurel wreaths.

### FIVE COURT OFFICES

After the hunters shall come on horseback a man with a verse inscription on which the five court offices shall be written: cupbearer, cook, barber, tailor, cobbler.   And Eberpach shall be vice-marshal and bear the verse plaque; this verse is yet to be composed.[10]

15
(So you may know who now appear,
Five court officials have we here:
Cupbearer, cook, and barber ride
With tailor and cobbler by their side.
Where'er the Emperor may be
They wait upon His Majesty.)

16
After him shall come five men riding in good order; the first shall bear a goblet, the second a ladle, the third a pair of barber's shears, the fourth a pair of tailor's shears, the fifth a last.
And they shall all be wearing laurel wreaths.

### Music[11]—Lutes and Viols

17
After them shall be depicted a low little car on small plough wheels; two elks shall draw the little car, and a little boy shall be the driver and shall bear the verse inscription.

18
And on the car shall be five lutenists and *rybeben*[12] players.

---

[10] The reader will remember that the verse which follows had not yet been written at the time our basic text was dictated by Maximilian in 1512.

[11] Many important musicians and composers were in the service of the music-loving Emperor.   Chief among them was Heinrich Isaac (1450?–1517), considered the first master of music in Germany, and famous for his polyphonic religious music and his settings of the song *Innsbruck, Ich Muss Dich Lassen*; he also served Lorenzo de' Medici in Florence as composer and as music teacher to his sons Pietro and Giovanni (later Pope Leo X).   Two other important musical luminaries of Maximilian's court, Hofhaimer and Slatkonia, are shown in person in woodcuts 22 and 26.   The beginnings of Viennese opera have been traced to the poetical pageants with music, singing, dance, and elaborate mythological apparatus staged for Maximilian by the humanist Conrad Celtis and others.   Electrola of Cologne has issued an excellent recording of music by Maximilian's composers in its series *Musik in Alten Städten und Residenzen*.   Old instruments such as those shown in the *Triumph* are used.

[12] This is the last known use of this instrument name, which is probably connected with "rebec."   Curt Sachs, in his *Real-Lexikon der Musikinstrumente* (Dover, 1963), identifies the instrument shown in the *Triumph* as an alto viola da gamba.

And their leader shall be Artus (master lutenist) and his verse, borne by the boy, shall read:
How he prepared the lutes and viols in the most artistic way for an entertainment by the Emperor's orders.

18
(Now lutes and viols harmonize
In elegant and courtly wise;
Thus bade by his Imperial might
Have I produced this fair delight,
Blending these tuneful instruments
As well befits such great events.)

The lutenists, viol players, and the boy shall all be wearing laurel wreaths.

### Music—Shawms, Trombones, Krummhorns

19
Then depict a low car on small plough wheels, drawn by two buffalo; a boy shall drive them and bear the leader's verse.
On the car shall be five shawm players, trombonists, and krummhorn[13] players.
And Neyschl (master trombonist) shall direct them, and his verse, borne by the boy, shall read:
How to the Emperor's joy and by his command he combined such diverse instruments in the merriest way.

20
(The trombone and the shawm adorn
The joyous sound of curving horn,
Each to the others well adjusted.
Since His Majesty entrusted
This musical command to me
I have performed quite frequently.)

All of them and the boy shall wear laurel wreaths.

---

[13] The krummhorn is the curved reed instrument shown here; its tone was similar to that of the modern English horn.

### Music—Regal and Positive

21 | Then shall be depicted a similar low little car on plough wheels, drawn by a camel;[14] a little boy shall drive it and bear the leader's verse.

On the car shall be a regal[15] and a positive organ and people playing them.

Their leader shall be Master Paul Hofhaimer,[16] organist, and his verse shall be as follows:

How by order of the Emperor he artistically increased and enlightened music.

22 | (Regal and positive I play with ease.
The organ, too, with many keys
I make resound with artful voices
So that each listener rejoices—
All with a master's understanding,
Our noble Emperor thus commanding.)

The boy and all of them shall wear laurel wreaths.

### Music—"Sweet Melody"

23 | Again depict a similar small low car with plough wheels, drawn by a dromedary; a boy shall drive it and bear the leader's verse.

On the car shall be the "sweet melody," that is:

24 | First, a *tämerlin*; a *quintern*; a large lute; a *rybeben*; a fiddle; a small *rauschpfeiffen*; a harp; a large *rauschpfeiffen*.[17]

---

[14] The animal in this woodcut seems to be the dromedary, while the beast in woodcut 23 would be the camel, at least in modern terminology.

[15] This is the small portable organ at the left; Hofhaimer is playing the positive.

[16] Hofhaimer (1459–1537), Maximilian's court organist at Innsbruck, is best remembered for his metrical setting of odes by Horace and for other works which were important precursors of the Protestant hymn style and homophonic developments in music.

[17] According to Curt Sachs, *op. cit.*, the *tämerlin* was a small drum, the *quintern* a type of guitar, and the *rauschpfeiffen* a reed instrument of the shawm family. The term *rauschpfeiffen* apparently occurs only in this description of the *Triumph*, and nowhere else.

The director's name and his verse are yet to be determined.

24 | (And now melodious music springs
From multifarious hums of strings.
By Emperor's wish the members are
The drum, the lute, the sweet guitar,
And harps and fifes both small and large.
To lead this consort is my charge.)

The boy and all of them shall be wearing laurel wreaths.

### Music—Choir

25 | Again depict a similar small low car with plough wheels, drawn by two wisents;[18] a boy shall drive them and bear the Kapellmeister's verse.

On the car should be the choir, and also cornet players and trombonists arranged in good order.

Herr Jorg Slakany (Bishop of Vienna)[19] shall be Kapellmeister and his verse shall be as follows:

How by the Emperor's instructions he arranged the choral singing most delightfully.

26 | (With voices high and low conjoint,
With harmony and counterpoint,
By all the laws of music moved,
My choir I constantly improved.
But not alone through my intent—
Give thanks to royal encouragement!)

Stewdl shall be leader of the trombonists, Augustin of the cornet players, and their verse, borne by a boy on the car, shall read thus:

How by the Emperor's instructions they attuned the trombones and cornets in most joyous manner.

---

[18] The wisent is the European bison; it is identified on the woodcut itself.

[19] George Slatkonia (1456–1522), Bishop of Vienna, humanist, poet, and composer, reestablished the Imperial court orchestra (*Hofkapelle*) along Renaissance lines (based on Burgundian and north Italian models) in 1498, and stayed on as its director. The orchestra was disbanded for reasons of economy by Charles V very shortly after Maximilian's death.

(The cornets and trombones we placed
So that the choral song they graced,
For His Imperial Majesty
Has often in such harmony
Taken great pleasure, and rightly so,
As we have had good cause to know.)

26  The boy and all of them shall wear laurel wreaths.
In the verses for the music one of the following words for "orders" or "instructions" shall be used in each so that there will be a distinction between them: *antzaigen, vnnderricht, beschaidt, vnnderweyssung, angebung.*

### JESTERS

27  After them shall come a man on horseback dressed as a jester, bearing a verse for the jesters and natural fools; he shall be Conrad von der Rosen.[20]
This verse is not yet ready.

(Assiduously always did I try
To keep buffoons in good supply,
Always to furnish the merriest jest—
To this one end I did my best.
And from my diligent employment
The Emperor derives enjoyment.)

28  After him shall come a small car drawn by two wild ponies; on it shall be these jesters: Lenz and Caspar, Bauer, Meterschy, and Dyweynndl.
And a boy shall be driver and all shall wear laurel wreaths.

### NATURAL FOOLS

29  After them depict yet another small car, on which shall be these natural fools: Gylyme, Pock, Gülichisch, Caspar, Hans Winter, Guggeryllis.

---

[20] Conrad von der Rosen was a personal friend and confidant of Maximilian, and is said to have saved his life more than once.

And a mule (two donkeys) shall draw the car, and a boy shall be driver.

29  (Another group is drawing near
Within this Triumph to appear:
These are the fools of the natural sort,
Very well known in the Emperor's court.
Their sayings and deeds without reason or rhyme
Have occasioned great laughter many a time.)

30  The jesters and natural fools and the two boys acting as drivers shall all be wearing laurel wreaths.

### MASQUERADE[21]

After them shall come a man on horseback in golden masquerade costume, dressed in the merriest manner.
Herr Peter von Altenhaus shall be master of the masquerade and his verse should read:
How by order of the Emperor he staged masquerades in an especially joyous manner and most honorably.

31  (Upon the Emperor's request
I made my joyous interest
The furtherance of masquerades
With all of art and humor's aids.
—But no licentiousness: instead
My wit is knightly and well bred.)

After him shall come on foot two ranks of mummers, five men in each rank, each carrying a burning torch.
The first rank shall be the golden masquerade, and shall wear short jackets in the old Swabian fashion.

---

[21] Maximilian was intensely fond of masquerades and introduced Burgundian and other foreign types to Austria. He commemorated his love for them in the *Freydal*, which remains the richest historical source on the subject for Maximilian's epoch. There were "characteristic" masquerades, in which the participants represented various nationalities, social classes, or personalities; and "grotesque" masquerades, in which fools, jongleurs, etc., were portrayed. The music was generally provided by fifes and drums. Monkeys, mock battles, and torch dances were popular elements of these courtly entertainments.

32
The second shall be the Spanish masquerade; they too shall wear short golden jackets with varied colors, and on their arms flying slit sleeves.

And all of them shall wear laurel wreaths.

### GEFECHT [22]

After them shall come a man on horseback, dressed gaily as a fighting master, and shall bear his verse inscription.

Herr Hans Hollywars shall be fighting master and his verse shall read:

How in noble manner he arranged the *Gefecht* at court by the Emperor's instructions.

33
> (With knightly joy, as you will note,
> The art of fencing I did promote
> With axe and halberd, staff and sword,
> As it did please my royal Lord;
> All done by rule and properly
> So the true basis you may see.)

Then the *Gefecht* shall follow, in groups of five men abreast in good order, as follows, all on foot.

Five men with (leather) flails.

34  Five men with quarterstaves.

35  Five men with lances.

36  Five men with halberds.

Five men with battleaxes.

37  Five men with bucklers; they shall have long swords unsheathed in their hands (men with rapiers and roundels).

38  Five men with shields; they shall have blades also unsheathed.

39  Five men (dressed in Hungarian style) with *pafessen* [23] (Hungarian shields); they shall have Hungarian maces.

40
Five men with (ordinary *Gefecht*) swords in the scabbards on their shoulders.

All shall be wearing laurel wreaths.

### TOURNEYERS [24]

After them shall come a man on horseback bearing a verse inscription, and wearing a tourneyer's armor.

The chief tourneyer shall be Herr Anthony von Yfan, and his verse shall read thus:

How by the Emperor's instructions he instituted tournaments at his court in knightly spirit.

41
> (Much of his time was nobly spent
> In the true knightly tournament,
> A source of valor and elation;
> Therefore, upon his instigation,
> With knightly spirit and bold heart
> I have improved this fighting art.)

42
After him five tourneyers abreast in good order on foot in full armor, wearing traditional helmets and not tourneying helmets, with their swords and lances, like mounted tourneyers, but with no round guards on their lances.

43
After them shall come five tourneyers on horseback abreast in good order, in full armor with their swords and lances and wearing traditional helmets.

These men shall all have laurel wreaths on their helmets.

### GESTECH [25]

44
After them shall come a man on horseback bearing a verse inscription and accoutred for *Rennen*, [26] with his head bare, wearing a

---

[22] These were combats on foot, considered beneath the notice of nobility or royalty until they were fostered by Maximilian, who took part in them himself. This type of sporting combat, in the generations that followed, was refined into the art of fencing.

[23] It was thought in Maximilian's day (and later) that the name *pafesse* was derived from the Bohemian word *pavéza*, meaning "shield"; but modern scholars lean toward a derivation from the Italian adjective *pavese*, "from the town of Pavia."

[24] Many suits of armor worn by Maximilian in these various types of sporting combat still exist. The *Freydal* contains descriptions and woodcut illustrations of many of the tourneys, jousts, and "courses" depicted in the *Triumph*. In tourneys, two parties of knights would engage; jousts (*Gestech* and *Rennen*) were between two individuals.

[25] This type of jousting used lances with coronals (three hooks) at their tip.

[26] *Rennen* ("course") was a type of jousting with pointed lances and lighter armor.

laurel wreath; he shall bear no shield, but shall have a golden chain around his neck.

Herr Wolfgang von Polhaim shall be master of *Rennen* and *Gestech*, and his verse shall read thus:

How knightly sports are nowhere in the world performed in such variety as he has caused them to be at court by order of the 44| Emperor.

(Always promoting new advances
In jousting with hooked or pointed lances,
Thanks to His Highness, I unfurled
Skills never seen in all the world.
These jousts in novel styles and ways
Have earned for me great fame and praise.)

Then shall be depicted the *Gestech* and *Rennen* as follows:
45 [ Italian *Gestech*,[27] five abreast in good order.
46 [ German *Gestech*,[28] five abreast in good order.
47 [ *Hohenzeuggestech*,[29] five abreast in good order.
*Gestech* in leg armor, five abreast in good order, the horses with a leather covering.

The participants in the *Gestech* shall bear their lances over their 48| heads and grasp the lances beneath the round guards.

The participants in the *Gestech* shall all wear laurel wreaths on their helmets and each shall have a crest on his helmet.

### RENNEN

49 [ Italian *Rennen* with *murneten*,[30] which are round and have circular guards, five men in good order.
50 [ *Bundrennen*,[31] five men in good order, with shields that jump up over their heads.

---

[27] In this type of joust the combatants rode toward each other on opposite sides of a low barrier; each man's object was to splinter his lance on his opponent's shield.

[28] This was the "ordinary German" joust with the object of unhorsing one's opponent.

[29] In this type the saddle was especially high and well protected; the object was to splinter the lance rather than to unhorse.

[30] This is the type of lance shown in the woodcut.

[31] Here the shields were so arranged that they would fly up over the head when properly struck; unhorsing was the object of this "course,"

51 [ *Geschifftrennen*,[32] five men on horseback in good order, with shields that jump up into the air in pieces.
*Helmletrennen*, five men in good order.
52 [ *Scheibenrennen*,[33] five men on horseback in good order, with beavers to their helmets and semicircular lance guards.
*Schildrennen*, five men in good order, with semicircular lance guards and also helmets with beavers.
53 [ *Pfannenrennen*,[34] five men in good order.
Herr Caspar Wintzer's *Rennen*, five men in good order, with semicircular lance guards and with shields.
Lance guard *Rennen* with small helmets, five men in good order.
54 [ *Feldrennen*,[35] five men in good order, with circular lance guards and small shields.
55 [ [*Schweifrennen*.[36]
[ *Wulstrennen*.[37]]
The participants in the *Rennen* shall bear their lances over their 56| head and grasp the lances above the semicircular guard.

The participants in the *Rennen* shall all be wearing laurel wreaths and adorned to suit their occupation.

### THE EMPEROR'S JOURNEY TO HIS BURGUNDIAN WEDDING

First three drummers in the Austrian colors.

Then three ranks of trumpeters, five in each rank, with the Austrian colors.

All shall wear laurel wreaths.

---

which was especially dangerous since the neck and chin were not protected by a beaver.

[32] Here the shield, when struck in the center, would separate into parts, which would fly up in the air.

[33] This was similar to the *Geschifftrennen*, but with circular shields.

[34] In this dangerous type, without armor, a metal plate on the chest was to be struck with the lance.

[35] This type, not shown in the *Freydal*, probably had splintering of the lance as its object.

[36] This was very similar to *Bundrennen*. The etymology is a matter of debate: from *Schweif*, "tail"? from *schweifen*, "to rove," indicating an oblique line of attack?

[37] This probably refers to the cushioned circlet around the heads of the combatants.

## The Austrian Territories

(A man on horseback; at the top of his lance, in the plaque:

> Austria's noble house now see
> Joined with that of Burgundy.
> For information full and clear
> Observe the arms that now appear,
> Royal escutcheons old and splendid,
> Through marriage marvelously blended.)

Then shall follow the Austrian hereditary territories, all borne in banners, not in gonfalons, by horsemen, and all with coats of arms, helmets, and crests.

And in any land in which the Emperor has waged war, the man bearing the banner shall wear armor, and the painter shall vary each one's armor in the old style.

And in any land in which the Emperor has not waged war, the banner-bearer shall not wear armor, but shall otherwise be clad most magnificently, each according to the costume of the territory; all shall wear laurel wreaths.

(Then a man on horseback bears the Austrian arms in a banner. Then a man on horseback bears the Old Austrian arms. Then a man on horseback bears the arms of Styria. Then one bears Carinthia.

57 [ Austria.[38] Old Austria. Styria.
58 [ Carinthia. Carniola. Swabia.
59 [ Alsace. Hapsburg. Tyrol.
60 [ Gorizia. Ferrete. Kyburg.
61 [ Region above the Enss. Burgau. Cilley.
62 [ Nellenburg. Hohenberg. Seckingen and Urach.
63 [ Glaris. Sunnenberg. Feldkirch.

64 [ Ortemburg. Echingen. Achalm.
65 [ Freiburg. Bregentz. Saulgau.
66 [ Walhausen. Ravensburg. Kirchberg.
67 [ Tockenburg. Andex. Friuli.
68 [ Trieste. Windischmark. Pordenone.
69 [ Trieberg. Razins. Torgau.
70 [ Reineck. Acht Gericht. Lieben.
71 [ Ehernberg. Weissenhorn. Hohenstauff.
72 [ Rapersweil. Black Forest. Neuburg on the Inn.
73 [ Duino. Oberwaldsee. [Unterwaldsee.]
74 [ Burgendt. Zeringen.
75 [ Bohemian inheritance. English inheritance.
76 [ [Portuguese inheritance.] Moravian inheritance.)

## Burgundian Fifers

77–79 [ After them shall come on horseback Burgundian fifers in the Burgundian colors with bombardons, shawms, and *rauschpfeiffen*.[39] And they shall all be wearing laurel wreaths.

## The Burgundian Territories

The Burgundian territories shall have banners, borne on horseback like the Austrian banners, but no one shall wear armor. Instead they shall be clad most magnificently and wear costly chains.

(Then men on horseback bear the arms of

80 [ Burgundy. Then one bears Lorraine. Brabant.
81 [ Limburg. Luxemburg. Gelderland.
82 [ Hainault. Burgundy.[40] Flanders. Arthois. Holland. Zeeland.[41]
83 [ Namur. Zutphen. Frisia.
84 [ Malines. Salins. Antwerp.

---

[38] There is no doubt that Burgkmair was responsible for woodcuts 1 through 56, many of which bear the initials HB. Woodcuts 57 through 88 comprise the next set, attributed by Meder (1932) to Albrecht Altdorfer on stylistic grounds. Benesch (1959) claims only numbers 57–61 and 80–84 of this group for Altdorfer. It is clear, however, that they were handled as a separate job in the division of labor on the *Triumph*: woodcut 58 bears the number 2 on it, 64 the number 8, 67–69 the numbers 11–13, 71–73 the numbers 15–17, 81 the number 24, 84 the number 28, and 87 the number 31.

---

[39] See note 17.

[40] This is the region Franche-Comté; the banner of the Duchy of Burgundy proper is shown in woodcut 80.

[41] The woodblock showing Arthois, Holland, and Zeeland is missing, and no impression of it exists, although there is evidence that it was cut.

85 [ Charolois. Maconois. Auxerrois.
86 [ Boulogne. Alost. Chimay.
87 [ Ostrevant. Arcus. Aussone.
88 [ Tenremonde. Franeker. Bethune.

### THE EMPEROR'S WEDDING [42]

89,  After them shall come two men on horseback bearing the
     Emperor's wedding; the inscription shall read thus:
90   Emperor Maximilian's wedding with the heiress-daughter of
     Burgundy.

### HERE FOLLOW THE WARS [43]

91–  Now a few *Landsknechte* [44] shall carry some castles and towns in
102  the ancient Roman style. [45]

---

[42] It will be seen at a glance that the woodcut version does not correspond to the plan for the miniatures. These two sheets (89 and 90) are the only ones still considered to be the work of Dürer. Dürer was also to have designed the woodcut for Maximilian's triumphal car (to be placed, presumably, in the center of the *Triumph*); a preparatory drawing exists, known in Dürer's output as the *kleiner Triumphwagen*. We also have from Dürer's hand a *grosser Triumphwagen*, dated 1522, which has never been included in any edition of the *Triumph*; this is a highly allegorical sequence of eight woodcuts in which numerous personifications of virtues attend the Emperor. There also exist six drawings by Dürer, apparently connected with the *Triumph*, of horsemen with various foreign trophies. Other work by Dürer for Maximilian includes marginal drawings in the *Prayer Book* (*Maximilians Gebetbuch*; Burgkmair, Baldung, and Cranach the Elder also contributed drawings; the *Gebetbuch* was dedicated to St. George, whose aid Maximilian invoked for a crusade—projected, but never undertaken—against the Turks); five woodcuts for the *Freydal* (1516); a woodcut portrait of the Emperor based on a drawing of 1518 (there is also a painting of Maximilian done in 1519 after the Emperor's death); and work on the *Triumphal Arch*: a number of the woodcuts as well as general artistic supervision of the project. Dover Publications will publish in 1963 a complete edition of Dürer's woodcuts, including his *grosser Triumphwagen*, his portrait of Maximilian, his woodcuts for the *Triumphal Arch*, and a double-page spread showing the entire *Arch*.—For an explanation of the words "Not in B." on woodcut 90, see the "Note on the Present Translation."

[43] Meder attributes woodcuts 91–110 to Dürer's pupil Hans Springinklee, who also worked on the *Arch*. Benesch gives Springinklee numbers 91–95 and 103–110. It is difficult to tell the wars apart in these woodcuts, but the lion in number 91 probably represents Venice, and the two women with joined hands in

### WAR IN HAINAULT

Then the war in Hainault shall be carried by a few soldiers with the inscription:
The war in Hainault and Picardy.

### BATTLE BEFORE THÉROUANNE [46]

91–  Then the battle before Thérouanne shall be carried by a few
102  soldiers with the inscription:
     The great battle before Thérouanne in the territory of Arthois.

### FIRST GELDERLAND WAR [47]

Then the first Gelderland war shall be carried by a few soldiers with the inscription:
The first conquest in Gelderland.

---

number 94 may symbolize Naples. Maximilian's significant use of artillery and siegecraft are apparent in these plates.

A sequence of eighteen round pen drawings of fourteen of Maximilian's wars and four of his hunts is still in existence. They date from Maximilian's lifetime and were probably done in Augsburg. Dörnhöffer saw sources for these drawings in the miniatures of the *Triumph*, in the many individual sheets with popular songs and woodcuts about Maximilian's wars, and in the frescos of contemporary wars and trophies that were painted on the arcades of a Fugger house in Augsburg in 1515 or 1516.

[44] Maximilian was the father of the *Landsknechte*, the first German regular troops. This Swabian mercenary infantry (modeled on the Swiss) made the German Empire an important military might.

[45] In ancient Roman triumphs paintings of battle scenes were carried; a version of such paintings is shown in Mantegna's *Triumph of Caesar*. The women with helmets and turreted headdresses in this part of the *Triumph of Maximilian* represent towns or regions.

[46] Battle before Thérouanne, at Guinegate (Enguinegatte): This was the famous "Battle of the Spurs," 1513, in which Maximilian, fighting at the head of English troops alongside Henry VIII, roundly defeated the French.

[47] Wars in Gelderland, Utrecht, Flanders, Liège, etc.: The Lowlands were part of the Burgundian holdings, of which Maximilian became master when he married Mary of Burgundy in 1477. After she died in 1482 in a fall from a horse, the Lowlands revolted for many years against their foreign overlord. For three months in 1488 Maximilian was held captive in the city of Bruges. The resistance of Gelderland was the most troublesome and continued longest.

### UTRECHT WAR

Then the Utrecht war shall be carried by a few soldiers with the inscription:
The Utrecht war.

### FIRST FLEMISH WAR

91–102 Then the first Flemish war shall be carried by a few soldiers with the inscription:
The first conquest of Flanders by the sword.

### LIÈGE WAR

Then the Liège war shall be carried by a few soldiers with the inscription:
The victory over the people of Liège.

### TROPHY CAR

103, 104 After these wars depict a trophy car with all sorts of Netherlandish and French weapons and banners of all colors, also all sorts of armor (with a man on horseback before).

### ROMAN CORONATION [48]

(A man on horseback with a lance, on it a plaque reading:

See His Imperial Majesty
Chosen in election free
O'er Holy Roman realm to reign
And Germany's kingdom to maintain:
Maximilian of world renown
Wearing the Imperial crown.)

---

[48] Maximilian's father, Frederick III, was the last Holy Roman Emperor to be crowned in Rome.  When Frederick died in 1493, Maximilian, who had been crowned "Roman King" (that is, King of Germany) in Aix-la-Chapelle in 1486, became de facto Holy Roman Emperor.  But the troubled state of Italy and his many wars did not permit him to visit Rome for the traditional coronation by the Pope.  Instead, in 1508 at Trent he proclaimed himself "Roman Emperor Elect," and was later confirmed in this title by the Pope.

After them shall come two men on horseback bearing the Emperor's Roman coronation; and the arms shall be the eagle with two heads, and the inscription shall read:
Emperor Maximilian's Roman coronation.
The "Roman woman" shall be dressed in Imperial robes and wear an Imperial crown.
Three finely dressed people (in honorable clothing of old style, one after another) shall bear the three Roman crowns on cushions before the Roman coronation: (the first) the straw crown (a wreath of rue; the second) the iron crown (a royal crown) and (the third) the golden crown (the Imperial crown).

### THE GERMAN KINGDOM

Then the German kingdom shall be borne on horseback; the Emperor shall sit like a Roman King; in the coat of arms shall be the eagle with one head, as borne by a Roman King.
In addition, there shall be depicted with their coats of arms the three houses Austria, Bavaria, and Saxony, and the three archbishoprics Magdeburg, Salzburg, and Bremen.
The "German woman" shall wear her hair loose and have a crown on her head.

### SECOND FLEMISH WAR

Then a few soldiers shall carry the Flemish war, and the inscription shall read:
The second conquest of Flanders.

### BURGUNDIAN WAR

Then a few soldiers shall carry the Burgundian war, and the inscription shall read:
The conquest of the two counties Burgundy and Arthois.

### AUSTRIAN WAR

Then a few soldiers shall carry the Austrian war, and the inscription shall read:
The conquest of a part of the Lower Austrian territories.

### HUNGARIAN WAR[49]

Then a few soldiers shall carry the Hungarian war, and the inscription shall read:
The adventurous Hungarian war.
(There follow coats of arms borne in banners on horseback. Hungary. Dalmatia. Croatia. Bosnia.)

### HUNGARIAN TROPHY CAR

Depict the trophy car (with four little banners) in Hungarian, Polish, Turkish, and Illyrian style.

### KING PHILIP'S WEDDING[50]

First there shall be borne in a banner on horseback the Spanish kingdoms, clad in attire and necklaces in the most costly fashion.
Castile. León. Aragon. Sicily. Jerusalem. Naples. Granada. Old Aragon. Old Granada. Toledo. Galicia. Valencia. Sardinia. Catalonia. Biscay. 1500 Islands.
Then two men on horseback shall bear King Philip's wedding, and the inscription shall read:
The wedding of King Philip, Archduke of Austria, son of Emperor Maximilian, with the heiress-daughter of Spain.

105

(As all these honors are reviewed
It would be false not to include,
Borne on its own triumphal carriage,
Our Archduke Philip's royal marriage;

The son of our Emperor gained the hand
Of the heiress to the Spanish land;
Then here to Austria she came
To honor Maximilian's fame.

105

On the plaque are painted Emperor Maximilian, King Philip, and the daughter of Spain in Imperial and royal attire and adornment, each with his coat of arms beside him.)

### SWISS WAR[51]

Then a few soldiers shall carry the Swiss war, and the inscription shall read:
The fierce Swiss war.

### NEAPOLITAN WAR

Then a few soldiers shall carry the Neapolitan war, and the inscription shall read:
The victorious aid brought to Naples.

### BAVARIAN WAR[52]

Then a few soldiers shall carry the Bavarian war, and the inscription shall read:
The Bavarian war.
(Three coats of arms borne in banners on three horses: Kufstein. Rothenburg. Kitzbühl.)

### BOHEMIAN BATTLE

Then a few soldiers shall carry the Bohemian battle, and the inscription shall read:
The Bohemian battle.

---

[49] This probably refers to Maximilian's expulsion of the Hungarians from Vienna and East Austrian territory after the death of their king Matthias Corvinus in 1490; at that time Maximilian fought on Hungarian soil also.

[50] Maximilian's greatest political successes were the dynastic marriages he arranged for his children and grandchildren. This marriage of his son, Philip the Handsome, Duke of Burgundy, to Juana, the daughter of Ferdinand and Isabella, soon made Spain a Hapsburg realm. Philip's son Charles became Charles I of Spain and as Charles V succeeded Maximilian as Holy Roman Emperor. Philip's other son Ferdinand was betrothed to Anne of Bohemia and Hungary at the Vienna "Congress of Princes" in 1515, and later brought those two regions into the Empire.

[51] The Swiss war of 1499 ended with the de facto (but permanent) loss to the Empire of the Swiss Confederation. Indeed, Maximilian's military career was by no means the sequence of unqualified victories suggested by the *Triumph*.

[52] This 1504 war over the inheritance of the Duke of Baiern-Landshut brought Kufstein, Rothenburg, and Kitzbühl into Hapsburg hands.

### BOHEMIAN TROPHY CAR

In the Bohemian trophy car shall be all sorts of Bohemian weapons, armor, and long shields, and Bohemian banners of all colors.

### SECOND GELDERLAND WAR

Then a few soldiers shall carry the second Gelderland war, and the inscription shall read:
The long second Gelderland war.

### THE RESTITUTION OF MILAN [53]

Then a few soldiers shall carry the restitution of Milan, and the inscription shall read:
The restitution of Milan to the Empire.

### VENETIAN WAR

Then a few soldiers shall carry the Venetian war, and the inscription shall read:
The great Venetian war.

### ITALIAN TROPHY CAR

Depict an Italian trophy car, on which are Lombardian and Italian weapons, armor, and banners.

---

[53] Wars in northern Italy: Maximilian's desperate effort to maintain a footing in Venetia, the southern Tyrol, and the hereditary Lombard lands of the Empire drained his treasury and diverted his attention from the pressing internal problems of his German lands. Medieval Imperial claims to Italian territories were being flouted by the active intervention of the French and Aragonese and the chicanery of the Venetians and the successive Popes. In 1496, Maximilian fought Charles VIII of France in northern Italy; his great Venetian war of 1509–1517 was a bewildering whirl of truces made and broken, of kaleidoscopic realignments of enmities and alliances with France, Venice, Spain, and the Pope. But the decisive victory of the new French king Francis I at Marignano in 1515 secured France's ascendancy in the area until after Maximilian's death.

### WARFARE PLAQUE

Then a verse inscription shall be borne on horseback, and the verse shall read:
In this triumph are shown the territories that His Imperial Majesty conquered by the sword; the towns, castles, fortifications, and manors are without number, and too many to be remembered by one person.

(The Emperor waged war constantly—
In Hungary, Hainault, Picardy,
In Arthois, Thérouanne, and Flanders,
With Austrians, with Gelderlanders;
Liège, Burgundy before him fell,
Naples, Utrecht, Milan, as well
As Swiss, Bohemian, Bavarian nations—
And Venice raised great lamentations.

Then two men shall bear a small galley.
Then two men shall bear a large galley.
Then two men shall bear a large skiff.
Four shall carry an inscription saying:
 Many a naval battle accomplished on sea and rivers.
And there shall be painted on it all sorts of ships large and small on water.)

### KINGDOM OF LOMBARDY

Then a man on horseback in full armor shall bear the Kingdom of Lombardy and the inscription:
The Kingdom of Lower Lombardy.

(Also the lower Lombard lands
Fell into our Emperor's hands.
He planned their fall by day and night
And took them by his army's might.
His glory will be ever green
Because his like was never seen.)

### The Six New Austrian and Burgundian Kingdoms [54]

First shall come on horseback the Archpalatinate.
Then the Archduchy.
Then the Kingdom of Austrasia.
Then the Kingdom of Lorraine.
Then the Kingdom of the Belgians.
Then the Kingdom of Slovania or the Wends.
Then the Kingdom of New Austrasia.
Then the Kingdom of Austria.
Represent in these banners the Holy Roman Empire, and then the Austrian territories related to the Empire.
The banners shall all be borne magnificently on horseback.

### Artillery [55]

After them shall come the artillery and the inscription shall read thus:
The famous artillery.
The people in this scene shall all wear laurel wreaths.

### Secular Treasure

After them shall come four men bearing the Imperial jewels and gold hoard, and the inscription shall read thus:
The jewels and the treasure for Imperial use.
The people shall all wear laurel wreaths.

### Sacred Treasure

After them shall come four men bearing the sacred treasure, and the inscription shall read thus:
The sacred treasure.
The people shall all wear laurel wreaths.

---

[54] Maximilian's plan to make separate kingdoms of these territories was never put into effect.

[55] As before noted, Maximilian took great pride in his accomplishments in artillery and siegecraft.

### Funerary Statues [56]

106

Now a man on horseback shall bear a plaque on which the following words shall be written:
The statues following represent the bold emperors, kings, archdukes, and dukes whose coat of arms and name Emperor Maximilian bears and whose land he rules.
The man on horseback shall also be wearing a laurel wreath.
Then the funerary statues shall be arranged one after the other with their coats of arms and borne on horseback, as on a litter, and the people leading the horses shall wear laurel wreaths.
The following are represented in the funerary statues:
Emperor Frederick III in Imperial regalia. [57]
Emperor Charles, in armor with his regalia over it.
Roman King Rudolph with armor and regalia.
Roman King Albrecht I, armor and regalia over it.
Roman King Albrecht II, no armor, only regalia.
King Arthur, full armor.
King Ladislaus, royally dressed in traditional style.
King Philip, dressed like King Ladislaus.

---

[56] Maximilian's interest in the genealogy of the Hapsburgs was intense. Historians in his service traced his lineage back to Hector of Troy (via the Franks) and even back to Noah. Burgkmair designed a sequence of woodcut portraits (about 1510–12) of 77 ancestors of the Emperor, handling admirably the difficult feat of lending individuality to so many worthies, most of whom were mere names. Leonhard Beck of Augsburg, to whom woodcuts 115–120 and 126 of the *Triumph* have been attributed, designed the woodcuts for the series *Saints of the Hapsburg Family* (*Heiligen aus der Sipp-, Mag-, und Schwagerschaft*). Probably the finest work of art to result from this interest of Maximilian was the bronze funerary monument to his Hapsburg ancestors in the Hofkirche at Innsbruck, on which such designers as Dürer and such sculptors as Peter Vischer the Elder labored; the project was not completed until more than thirty years after the Emperor's death. Maximilian also planned a monument to previous dynasties of Holy Roman Emperors in the cathedral of Speier, burial place of the Emperors; this was never executed.

[57] Frederick III (reigned 1440–93), father of Maximilian, was perhaps the most ineffectual of all Holy Roman Emperors. His bloody feuds with his own clan members only aggravated the complete weakness in internal and foreign affairs that culminated in his loss of Vienna to the Hungarians (see note 49). One of the earliest accomplishments of Maximilian's reign (whether he is to be credited with it or not) was the proclamation in 1495 of the *ewiger Landfriede*, or "everlasting domestic peace," which put an end for the duration to internecine wrangles within Hapsburg territories.

King Stephen, dressed in old royal fashion.

King John of Portugal, dressed in old royal fashion.

Archduke Frederick of Austria, dressed like an archduke, with an appropriate scepter in his hand.

Archduke Sigmund of Austria, dressed like an archduke, with an appropriate scepter in his hand.

Duke Philip of Burgundy, dressed like a duke.

Duke Charles of Burgundy, dressed like a duke.

Duchess Kunegund.

Duchess Margaret.[58]

Duchess Zymburg.[59]

Duchess Mary.

Roman Queen Elizabeth.

Roman Queen Blanca Maria.[60]

Roman Empress Leonora.[61]

[Series of funerary statues on woodcuts:

106 [ Frederick III.

Charlemagne.

Clovis I.

107 Stephen, King of Hungary.

Rudolph I.

Odobert, King of Provence.

King Arthur of England.

108 King John of Portugal.

Godfrey of Bouillon, King of Jerusalem.

Albrecht, Roman King.

Albrecht, Roman King and King of Hungary and Bohemia.

109 Ladislaus, King of Hungary and Bohemia.

King Ferdinand of Spain.

King Philip of Castile.

110 Leopold the Holy, Margrave of Austria.

Archduke Sigmund of Austria.

Duke Charles of Burgundy.[62]]

---

## PRISONERS [63]

(A man on horseback, and above, in the plaque he bears:

> The members of this captive band
> Are prisoners from every land
> Where Maximilian waged war—
> The battles were all shown before.
> Marching in this Triumph now,
> To his Imperial will they bow.)

111, 112 [ After him shall follow the prisoners (from all sorts of countries); a few soldiers shall lead the prisoners and around the prisoners shall be a chain.

All the soldiers in this Triumph, with no exceptions, shall wear full hose and doublets and laurel wreaths on their heads.

All horsemen in this Triumph, also with no exceptions, shall also wear laurel wreaths.

113, 114 [ (Then follow two groups, ten people in each, every man carrying a statue of a woman with angel's wings; each of these women carries a palm or some other symbol of triumph.)

## IMPERIAL TRUMPETERS [64]

115– 117 [ After them shall come on horseback a goodly number of trumpeters and drummers with the Imperial flags on their trumpets, and wearing laurel wreaths.

## HERALDS

118– 120 [ After them shall come on horseback a number of heralds with their heralds' jackets (in groups of five in a rank, each with a yellow staff and bearing a particular coat of arms, like heralds) and wearing laurel wreaths.

---

[58] Daughter of Maximilian by Mary of Burgundy.

[59] Mother of Frederick III, of Polish birth.

[60] Bianca Maria Sforza, Maximilian's second wife, niece of Lodovico Moro of Milan; this was a purely political marriage.

[61] Maximilian's mother, a Portuguese princess; she is said to have transmitted her love of chivalrous romances to her son.

[62] Charles the Bold, father of Maximilian's wife Mary.

[63] Both Meder and Benesch assign to Burgkmair the two sheets of prisoners and the two sheets of men carrying statues of women. Numbers 112–114 bear the initials HB.

[64] Both Meder and Benesch assign to Leonhard Beck the seven woodcuts 115–120 and 126.

(A triumphal car, and on it five female figures in Imperial, royal, and princely attire; in front four horses with white-clad boys on them. Some coats of arms shall also be on the car.)

121 [A king and queen [65]—perhaps Roman King Philip and his consort Juana—on horseback, in royal dress, with scepters. Six men of the bodyguard go before and behind them with lances.

122 A princess on horseback. She is magnificently dressed, wears a crown, and holds a small whip in her hand. Two noble gentlemen lead her horse by the bridle. Behind her, also on horseback, follow two ladies-in-waiting, splendidly adorned, and accompanied by three halberdiers.

123 A man on horseback with a verse inscription plaque, and behind him two men of foreign nations, each leading a saddled and caparisoned horse.

124, 125 Two ranks of five men, all in costumes of various nations, each likewise leading a saddled and caparisoned horse.]

## IMPERIAL BANNER

After them the Imperial banner shall be borne on horseback by Christoph Schenk, wearing armor and a laurel wreath; it shall be the eagle with two heads.

## IMPERIAL SWORD

Then the sword shall be borne on horseback by the Imperial marshal, wearing a laurel wreath and richly dressed.

---

[65] Woodcuts 121–125, given these numbers by Schestag, were, along with Schestag's 89 and 90 (the two by Dürer), placed at the end of Bartsch's edition and described by him in a supplement to the descriptive text; the sixteenth-century texts do not mention them, although they were surely cut for the *Triumph*. Schestag does not make it clear where in this text he would have wished to place the description of these five sheets; I have chosen this place as the most convenient and proper. Numbers 121 and 122 are ascribed to Springinklee by Meder; both Meder and Benesch credit Burgkmair with 123–125, and these three do, in fact, show the initials HB.

## THE EMPEROR'S TRIUMPHAL CAR [66]

Then shall be brought the Emperor's triumphal car, depicted with the utmost richness; on this triumphal car shall be seated the Emperor in his Imperial dress and majesty. With him on the triumphal car shall be, in order: his first wife, also King Philip and his wife, and Margaret, and King Philip's children; Duke Charles shall be wearing a crown.

(And the triumphal car shall be drawn by finely adorned horses, as befits an Imperial triumphal car.)

## PRINCES

Then shall come a man riding a finely adorned horse, bearing a verse inscription, and wearing a laurel wreath; in the plaque shall be written these words:

The chosen princes.

(The Emperor has chosen for their great worth
The princes of illustrious birth
Who follow now in brave array
And high on horseback make their way.
The battle-won kingdoms and princely lands
Are shown in the banners they hold in their hands.)

After him shall come the princes in groups of five abreast, with their banners, as they are included by name in the following list, and each man's name shall be written on the banner he carries.

Duke Frederick of Saxony.
Duke Albrecht of Bavaria.
Duke Albrecht of Saxony. [67]
Duke Otto of Bavaria.
Duke Henry of Brunswick.
(Count Palatine Frederick of Bavaria.)

---

[66] For Dürer's work on the Emperor's Triumphal Car, see note 42.

[67] Albrecht (Albert) of Saxony was Maximilian's chief general in the Lowland campaigns; he continued to put down the uprisings after Maximilian returned to Austria in 1489.

Duke Christoph of Bavaria.
Duke Eric of Brunswick.
Duke William of Juliers.
Margrave Frederick of Brandenburg.
Landgrave William der Mittler of Hesse.
Margrave Christoph of Baden.
Margrave Sigmund of Brandenburg.
Margrave Albrecht of Brandenburg.
Margrave Casimir of Brandenburg.
Prince Rudolph of Anhalt.
The Prince of Chimay.
The princes shall all be wearing laurel wreaths.

### Counts

Then shall come a finely attired man on horseback, wearing a laurel wreath and carrying a verse inscription in which these words are written:
The renowned counts and barons.

> (No less the honor and circumstance
> For the counts and barons who now advance;
> Granting their lofty birth its due,
> They gave the Emperor service true.
> Knightly precepts they held ever dear
> And fought for the Empire many a year.)

Then shall come on horseback the counts and barons, in groups of five abreast, with their banners, as they are included with their banners in the following list, and each one's name shall be written on his banner.
Count Albrecht of Zorn. Count Frederick of Zorn. Count Eytlfridrich of Zorn. Count Ulrich of Werdemberg. Count Henry of Fürstemberg. The Counts of Nassau. The Counts of Frangipan.

### Barons

The Barons of Polhaim. The Baron of Fay. Eberhard, Baron of Aremberg. Pfeffers. Jacob, Baron of Luxemburg. Jan, Baron of Berg. Veit, Baron of Wolkenstein. Heyg of Milin. The Barons of Lanno. Cornelius, Baron of Berg. Franciscus de Montibus.

Dietrich, Baron of Tschernaho. Mörsberg. Sir Christoph Weytmulner. The counts and barons shall all be wearing laurel wreaths.

### Knights

Then shall come a finely attired man on horseback, wearing a laurel wreath and carrying a verse inscription in which these words shall be written:
The praiseworthy knights.

> (The Emperor's bold heart at all times
> Toward heights of knightly virtue climbs,
> And so with all his will and might
> He cherishes each worthy knight
> Who fearlessly his life will yield
> To serve him on the battlefield.)

Then shall come the knights on horseback, in groups of five abreast, each bearing a banner with his name on it; the names of these knights follow:
Herr Reinprecht of Reichemberg. Herr Friedrich Kappeler. Herr Wilhelm von Pappenhaim. Herr Jost von Alein. Herr Hans Teschitz. Herr Ebolt von Liechtenstein. Gallin von Pergen. Herr Jan Salesar. Herr Sytich Zebitz. Herr Melchior Massmünster.[68] Herr Reinhard May. Herr Jorg von Ebenstain. Herr Ulrich Anckenreuter. Philip von Freiburg. Herr Joss Brantner. Louis de Vaudre. Herr Sixt Trautsun. Jacob von Embs. Franz Schenck. Charlot de Saveuse. Herr Heinrich Humpis. Alferat. Falkensteiner. Jacob Valera. Christoph Truchsess von Stetten. Herr Jacob Halder. Herr Lienhard Veter.
And they shall all be wearing laurel wreaths.

---

[68] Massmünster, one of Maximilian's diplomatic staff, negotiated with Denmark and some of the German princes in an attempt to win aid against Poland, which was threatening to engulf the East Prussian lands of the Teutonic Order. In preparation for a conflict in this quarter, Maximilian signed an offensive and defensive alliance with Russia at Gmunden, Austria, on August 4, 1514. This is the first record of a Russian embassy to a Western power. (Burgkmair designed a color woodcut of Maximilian's meeting with the Russians.) The next year, however, in order to smooth the way for the marriage of his grandson Ferdinand to Anne of Bohemia and Hungary, Maximilian left Danzig and the Teutonic Order to their fate.

## MERITORIOUS SOLDIERS

Then shall come a man on foot bearing a verse inscription and wearing a laurel wreath; in the verse plaque these words shall be written:

The meritorious soldiers.

126

(The worthy soldiers in every war
With knightly spirit hunger for
Fame everlasting and honors grand
Through the Emperor's counsel and command.
And so his praise is justly sung
By rich and poor, by old and young.

Then follow two ranks of arquebusiers, five men in each.)

Then shall come these soldiers on foot, in groups of five abreast, with their lances; each one shall have his name written on his clothing or on a small flag attached to his laurel wreath. The names follow:

Martin Swartz. Mang von Schafhausen. János. Juan Talsat, Spaniard. Peter von Winterthur. Peter Plarer. Hans Wanner. Richard Vantos, Englishman. Kunz Hechinger. Weydehart. Hein Oterle, Swiss. Rap von Cili. Jorg von Ulm. Hans Ebwein. Lynnsl. Fleck, Swiss. Loflinger. Peter Wunderlich. Black Hans. Peter Rörl. Jacob Müllner. Ergot. Spagörl, drummer. Jeckel, player of the long fife.

(Then three standard-bearers and two alongside them with halberds; the three standard-bearers carry in their banners the Imperial, Austrian, and Burgundian coats of arms.

Another rank of halberdiers.

127 Two more ranks with long lances,[69] over the first rank their names.

Another two ranks of arquebusiers.)

128 [Two ranks with swords.]

And they shall all be wearing laurel wreaths.

---

[69] This sheet and the following are attributed to Hans Schäufelein (1480?–1539?), who was responsible for most of the woodcuts in the *Theuerdank*.

## WAGON BARRICADE [70]

After them shall come a man on horseback, wearing a laurel wreath and carrying a verse inscription; Herr Hans Wülfersdorfer shall be master of the wagon barricade; his verse is still to be written.

(With skill this wagon barricade
I formed in the field, as here displayed,
Circling and closing in the swiftest way
So none of the men would go astray.
Inside now are erected tents
And other martial monuments.)

Then the wagon barricade shall be brought.

And the people in the wagon barricade shall all be wearing laurel wreaths.

## PEOPLE OF CALICUT [71]

129–
131

After them shall come a man of Calicut (naked, with a loincloth), mounted and carrying a verse inscription, wearing a laurel wreath; on the plaque shall be written these words:

These people are subject to the previously shown praiseworthy crowns and houses.

---

[70] This military maneuver consisted in making a circle of wagons, much like the protective ring of Conestogas in Western films.

[71] It has always been clear that the three sheets of "people of Calicut" are the work of Burgkmair (note the HB on the elephant's neckpiece). Some time during the first decade of the sixteenth century Burgkmair had provided six woodcut illustrations for the travel reports of the Tyrolese Balthasar Springer (or Sprenger), who, along with one Hans Mayr, was the first German to visit India; he and Mayr, backed by funds of the Fuggers and other merchants of Augsburg and Nuremberg, had sailed to the East on a Portuguese vessel. Springer's reports are full of rich and accurate geographical and ethnographical observations; Burgkmair's woodcuts include many exotic human and animal types. Perhaps the connection with Springer explains why Burgkmair's elephant, though clearly not drawn from life, is so much more realistic than the elephants in Mantegna's *Triumph of Caesar*, which perpetuate the widespread medieval conception of beasts with tiny heads and flaring trunks. The "people of Calicut" who are dressed in feathers are more reminiscent of American Indians; and, in fact, the New York Public Library possesses a woodcut (of much poorer

(The Emperor in his warlike pride,
Conquering nations far and wide,
Has brought beneath our Empire's yoke
The far-off Calicuttish folk.
Therefore we pledge him with our oath

129–
131   Lasting obedience and troth.)

Then shall come on foot the people of Calicut.
(One rank with shields and swords.
One rank with spears.
Two ranks with English bows and arrows.
All are naked like Indians or dressed in Moorish fashion.)
They shall all be wearing laurel wreaths.

### BAGGAGE TRAIN [72]

After them shall come on horseback Hieronymus von Herem-
berg,[73] bearing a verse inscription; he shall be master of the baggage
train; his verse is yet to be composed.

132–
137

(The baggage train and army's gear
Guarded by those who now appear,
I led in order excellent.
My efforts were quite evident.
I kept the army fully free
From pilferage and thievery.)

---

quality) executed in Augsburg around 1505 which portrays savages in Brazil.
The primitive inhabitants of the newly discovered East and West "Indies"
were popular figures in several live and pictured triumphs of the sixteenth
century. Probably the height of "exoticism" was achieved in French king
Henri II's *entrée* into Rouen in 1550, for which a sizable Brazilian forest, complete
with authentic flora, fauna, and naked savages, imported and domestic, was
erected on the banks of the Seine. To return to our *Triumph of Maximilian*, it
is clear at any rate that the Emperor had not "conquered" the Indians as he
claims; I assume this was a high-spirited extension of the theme of conquest
that is, after all, quite appropriate to a triumph.

[72] Meder attributes the baggage train sequence to Wolf Huber; Benesch
assigns it to Altdorfer. Both were painters and illustrators belonging to the
"Danube School," one of whose characteristics was the rich use of landscape
which appears here and nowhere else in the *Triumph*. Baldass (1923) considered
the baggage train to be the work of Hans Dürer, brother of Albrecht. These
woodcuts would probably have come at the end of the completed *Triumph*.

[73] On woodcut 132, see the "Note on the Present Translation."

132–
137   Then shall be arranged the baggage train (with all sorts of
followers and various activities) on horse and foot in sequence
according to the way of baggage trains; all shall be wearing laurel
wreaths.

### END OF THE TRIUMPH

### SELECT LIST OF BOOKS AND ARTICLES CONSULTED

ASPLAND, ALFRED, ed., *The Triumphs of the Emperor Maximilian I,
with Woodcuts Designed by Hans Burgmair, Reproduced by the Holbein
Society*, Manchester and London; text volume, 1875; 2 vol. of plates,
1873.

BALDASS, LUDWIG, *Der Künstlerkreis Kaiser Maximilians*, Anton
Schroll & Co., Vienna, 1923; referred to in notes as Baldass (1923).

[BARTSCH, ADAM, ed.], *Kaiser Maximilians I Triumph: Le
Triomphe de l'Empereur Maximilien I en une suite de cent trente cinq
planches gravées en bois d'après les Desseins de Hans Burgmair, accom-
pagnées de l'ancienne description dictée par l'empereur à son secrétaire Marc
Treitzsaurwein, Imprimé à Vienne chez Matthias André Schmidt,
Imprimeur de la Cour, et se trouve a Londres chez J. Edward, Pall Mall,
1796* (Third Edition of *Triumph*).

BENESCH, OTTO, "Maximilien, empereur gothique et renaissant,"
*Oeil*, **58**, 16–23 and 68, October, 1959.

BIENER, CLEMENS, "Waffennamen zur Zeit Maximilians I,"
*Wörter und Sachen*, **16**, 47–60, 1934.

CHARTROU, JOSÈPHE, *Les entrées solennelles et triomphales à la
Renaissance (1484–1551)*, Presses Universitaires de France, Paris,
1928.

CHMELARZ, EDUARD, "Die Ehrenpforte des Kaisers Maximilian
I," *Jahrbuch der Kunsthistorischen Sammlungen des Allerhöchsten Kaiserhauses*, **4**, 289–319, 1886.

CLEPHAN, R. COLTMAN, *The Tournament: Its Periods and Phases*,
Methuen and Co., London, 1919.

DODGSON, CAMPBELL, "A German-Russian Alliance in 1514,"
*Burlington Magazine*, **76**, 139–144, May, 1940.

DÖRNHÖFFER, FRIEDRICH, "Ein Cyclus von Federzeichnungen mit Darstellungen von Kriegen und Jagden Maximilians I," *Jahrbuch der Kunsthistorischen Sammlungen des Allerhöchsten Kaiserhauses*, **18**, 1–55 and 274–276, 1897.

EAMES, WILBERFORCE, "Description of a Wood Engraving Illustrating the South American Indians (1505)," *Bulletin of the New York Public Library*, **26**, 755–760, September, 1922.

IVINS, W. M., JR., "Burgkmair's Prints in the Museum," *Metropolitan Museum Bulletin*, **32**, 251–255, November, 1937.

KOCZIRZ, ADOLF, "Die Auflösung der Hofmusikkapelle nach dem Tode Kaiser Maximilians I," *Zeitschrift für Musikwissenschaft*, 531–540, August-September, 1931.

KURTH, WILLI, ed., *The Complete Woodcuts of Albrecht Dürer*, Dover Publications, Inc., New York, 1963.

LEITNER, QUIRIN VON, ed., *Freydal, des Kaisers Maximilian I Turniere und Mummereien*, A. Holzhausen, Vienna, 1880–82.

*Maximilian I, 1459–1519, Ausstellung, Österreichische Nationalbibliothek, Graphische Sammlung Albertina, Kunsthistorisches Museum (Waffensammlung), 23. Mai bis 30. September 1959*, Österreichische Nationalbibliothek, Vienna, 1959; section on *Triumph* by Otto Benesch and Alice Strobl; referred to in notes as Benesch (1959).

MEDER, JOSEPH, *Dürer-Katalog: Ein Handbuch über Albrecht Dürers Stiche, Radierungen, Holzschnitte, deren Zustände, Ausgaben und Wasserzeichen*, Verlag Gilhofer und Ranschburg, Vienna, 1932; referred to in notes as Meder (1932).

PARKER, K. T., "Five Mounted Drummers, from the Triumphal Procession of the Emperor Maximilian," *Old Master Drawings*, **6**, 35–36, September, 1931.

REMINGTON, P., "Two Gobelins Tapestries," *Metropolitan Museum Bulletin*, **30**, 155–158, August, 1935.

ROMMEL, OTTO, ed., *Wiener Renaissance* (Vol. 1 of series *Klassiker der Wiener Kultur*), Bellaria-Verlag, Vienna-Zurich, n.d. [1946?].

SACHS, CURT, *Real-Lexikon der Musikinstrumente: zugleich ein Polyglossar für das gesamte Instrumentengebiet*, 2nd revised and enlarged edition, Dover Publications, Inc., New York, 1963.

SCHESTAG, FRANZ, ed., "Kaiser Maximilian I. Triumph," *Jahrbuch der Kunsthistorischen Sammlungen des Allerhöchsten Kaiserhauses*, **I**, 154–181, 1883; plus pictorial supplement, *Triumph des Kaisers Maximilian I*, Adolf Holzhausen, Vienna, 1883–84 (Fourth Edition of *Triumph*).

SCHULZE, FRANZ, *Balthasar Springers Indienfahrt 1505/06: Wissenschaftliche Würdigung der Reiseberichte Springers zur Einführung in den Neudruck seiner "Meerfahrt" vom Jahre 1509* (No. 8 of series *Drucke und Holzschnitte des XV. und XVI. Jahrhunderts in getreuer Nachbildung*), J. H. E. Heitz, Strassburg, 1902.

THODE, HENRY, *Mantegna* (No. 27 of series *Künstler-Monographien*), Velhagen und Klasing, Bielefeld and Leipzig, 1897.

ZOEGE VON MANTEUFFEL, K[urt], *Der Deutsche Holzschnitt: Sein Aufstieg im XV. Jahrhundert und seine grosse Blüte in der ersten Hälfte des XVI. Jahrhunderts* (Vol. 1 of series *Kunstgeschichte in Einzeldarstellungen*), Hugo Schmidt Verlag, Munich, 1921.

*The Plates*

2

I

4

6

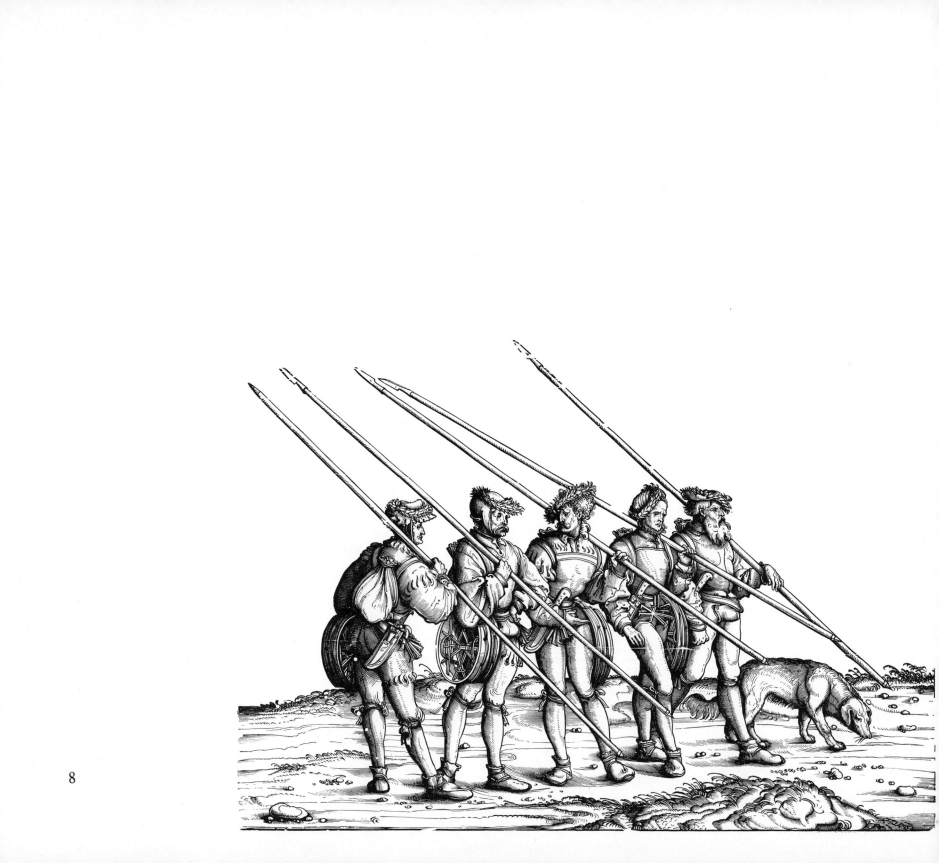

8

7

10

12

II

14

13

16

18

17

20

19

24

23

WISEND ·

25

27

29

32

31

34

33

35

38

37

40

39

42

41

43

46

45

48

47

50

49

51

54

53

55

59

61

63

70

69

71

74

73

78

77

81

83

86

85

122
131

130

123

132
Not in B.

*General View of the "Triumph"*

10     9     8     7     6

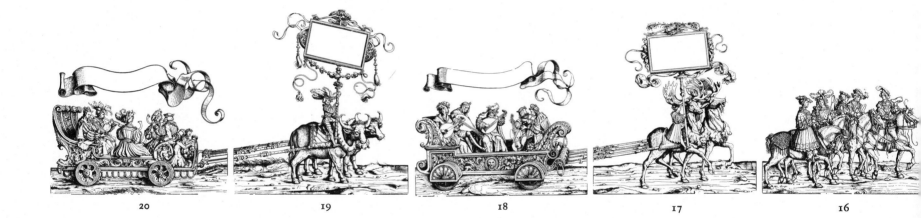

20     19     18     17     16

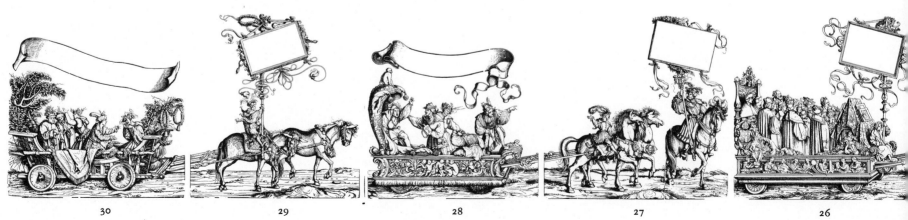

30     29     28     27     26

5  4  3  2  1

15  14  13  12  11

25  24  23  22  21

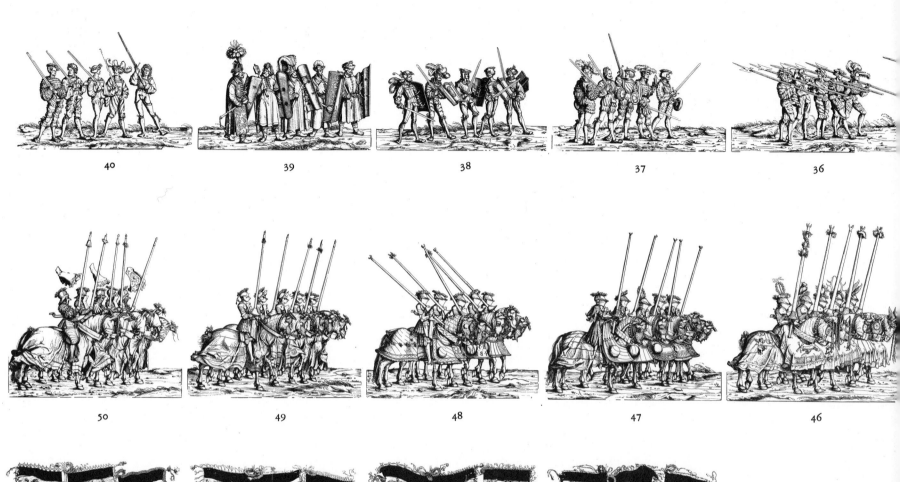

40                39                38                37                36

50                49                48                47                46

60                59                58                57                56

35       34       33       32       31

45       44       43       42       41

55       54       53       52       51

70        69        68        67        66

80        79        78        77        76

90        89        88        87        86

65         64         63         62         61

75         74         73         72         71

85         84         83         82         81

100         99         98         97         96

110         109         108         107         106

120         119         118         117         116

95     94     93     92     91

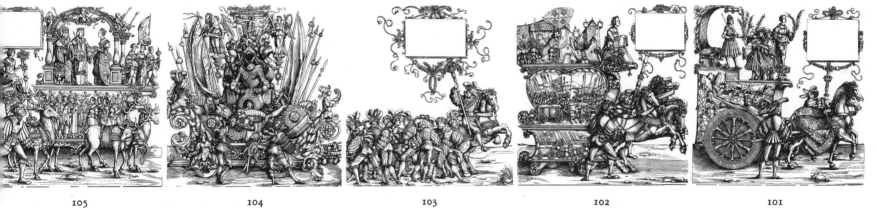

105     104     103     102     101

115     114     113     112     111

130                129                128                127                126

137                136

125   124   123   122   121

135   134   133   132   131

Dover Books on Art

# Dover Books on Art

*VASARI ON TECHNIQUE, G. Vasari.* Pupil of Michelangelo, outstanding biographer of Renaissance artists reveals technical methods of his day. Marble, bronze, fresco painting, mosaics, engraving, stained glass, rustic ware, etc. Only English translation, extensively annotated by G. Baldwin Brown. 18 plates. xxiv + 328pp. 5⅜ x 8.　　　　　T717 Paperbound $2.00

*FOOT-HIGH LETTERS: A GUIDE TO LETTERING, M. Price.* 28 15½ x 22½" plates, give classic Roman alphabet, one foot high per letter, plus 9 other 2" high letter forms for each letter. 16 page syllabus. Ideal for lettering classes, home study. 28 plates in box.　　　　　T239 $6.00

*A HANDBOOK OF WEAVES, G. H. Oelsner.* Most complete book of weaves, fully explained, differentiated, illustrated. Plain weaves, irregular, double-stitched, filling satins; derivative, basket, rib weaves; steep, broken, herringbone, twills, lace, tricot, many others. Translated, revised by S. S. Dale; supplement on analysis of weaves. Bible for all handweavers. 1875 illustrations. 410pp. 6⅛ x 9¼.　　　　　T209 Clothbound $5.00

*JAPANESE HOMES AND THEIR SURROUNDINGS, E. S. Morse.* Classic describes, analyzes, illustrates all aspects of traditional Japanese home, from plan and structure to appointments, furniture, etc. Published in 1886, before Japanese architecture was contaminated by Western, this is strikingly modern in beautiful, functional approach to living. Indispensable to every architect, interior decorator, designer. 307 illustrations. Glossary. 408pp. 5⅝ x 8⅜.　　　　　T746 Paperbound $2.00

*THE DRAWINGS OF HEINRICH KLEY.* Uncut publication of long-sought-after sketchbooks of satiric, ironic iconoclast. Remarkable fantasy, weird symbolism, brilliant technique make Kley a shocking experience to layman, endless source of ideas, techniques for artist. 200 drawings, original size, captions translated. Introduction. 136pp. 7¾ x 10¾.　T24 Paperbound $1.85

*COSTUMES OF THE ANCIENTS, Thomas Hope.* Beautiful, clear, sharp line drawings of Greek and Roman figures in full costume, by noted artist and antiquary of early 19th century. Dress, armor, divinities, masks, etc. Invaluable sourcebook for costumers, designers, first-rate picture file for illustrators, commercial artists. Introductory text by Hope. 300 plates. 5⅝ x 8⅜. 348pp.　　　　　T21 Paperbound $2.00

*ART ANATOMY, Dr. William Rimmer.* One of the few books on art anatomy that are themselves works of art, this is a faithful reproduction (rearranged for handy use) of the extremely rare masterpiece of the famous 19th century anatomist, sculptor, and art teacher. Beautiful, clear line drawings show every part of the body—bony structure, muscles, features, etc. Unusual are the sections on falling bodies, foreshortenings, muscles in tension, grotesque personalities, and Rimmer's remarkable interpretation of emotions and personalities as expressed by facial features. It will supplement every other book on art anatomy you are likely to have. Reproduced clearer than the lithographic original (which sells for $500 on up on the rare book market.) Over 1,200 illustrations. xiii + 153pp. 7¾ x 10¾.　　　　　T908 Paperbound $2.00

*BYZANTINE ART AND ARCHAEOLOGY, O. M. Dalton.* Still most thorough work in English on Byzantine art forms throughout ancient and medieval world. Analyzes hundreds of pieces, covers sculpture, painting, mosaic, jewelry, textiles, architecture, etc. Historical development; specific examples; iconology and ideas; symbolism. A treasure-trove of material about one of most important art traditions, will supplement and expand any other book in area. Bibliography of over 2500 items. 457 illustrations. 747pp. 6⅛ x 9¼.　　　T776 Clothbound $8.50

*STICKS AND STONES, Lewis Mumford.* An examination of forces influencing American architecture: the medieval tradition in early New England, the classical influence in Jefferson's time, the Brown Decades, the imperial facade, the machine age, etc. "A truly remarkable book," SAT. REV. OF LITERATURE. 2nd revised edition. 21 illus. xvii + 240pp. 5⅜ x 8.　　　　　T202 Paperbound $1.60

*THE AUTOBIOGRAPHY OF AN IDEA, Louis Sullivan.* The architect whom Frank Lloyd Wright called "the master" records the development of the theories that revolutionized America's skyline. 34 full-page plates of Sullivan's finest work. New introduction by R. M. Line. xiv + 335pp. 5⅜ x 8.　　　　　T281 Paperbound $2.00

*THE MATERIALS AND TECHNIQUES OF MEDIEVAL PAINTING, D. V. Thompson.* An invaluable study of carriers and grounds, binding media, pigments, metals used in painting, al fresco and al secco techniques, burnishing, etc. used by the medieval masters. Preface by Bernard Berenson. 239pp. 5⅜ x 8.　　　　　T327 Paperbound $1.85

*HANDBOOK OF DESIGNS AND DEVICES, C. P. Hornung.* A remarkable working collection of 1836 basic designs and variations, all copyright-free. Variations of circle, line, cross, diamond, swastika, star, scroll, shield, many more. Notes on symbolism. "A necessity to every designer who would be original without having to labor heavily," ARTIST AND ADVERTISER. 204 plates. 240pp. 5⅜ x 8.      T125 Paperbound $1.90

*THE UNIVERSAL PENMAN, George Bickham.* Exact reproduction of beautiful 18th-century book of handwriting. 22 complete alphabets in finest English roundhand, other scripts, over 2000 elaborate flourishes, 122 calligraphic illustrations, etc. Material is copyright-free. "An essential part of any art library, and a book of permanent value," AMERICAN ARTIST. 212 plates. 224pp. 9 x 13¾.      T20 Clothbound $10.00

*AN ATLAS OF ANATOMY FOR ARTISTS, F. Schider.* This standard work contains 189 full-page plates, more than 647 illustrations of all aspects of the human skeleton, musculature, cutaway portions of the body, each part of the anatomy, hand forms, eyelids, breasts, location of muscles under the flesh, etc. 59 plates illustrate how Michelangelo, da Vinci, Goya, 15 others, drew human anatomy. New 3rd edition enlarged by 52 new illustrations by Cloquet, Barcsay. "The standard reference tool," AMERICAN LIBRARY ASSOCIATION. "Excellent," AMERICAN ARTIST. 189 plates, 647 illustrations. xxvi + 192pp. 7⅞ x 10⅝.      T241 Clothbound $6.00

*AN ATLAS OF ANIMAL ANATOMY FOR ARTISTS, W. Ellenberger, H. Baum, H. Dittrich.* The largest, richest animal anatomy for artists in English. Form, musculature, tendons, bone structure, expression, detailed cross sections of head, other features, of the horse, lion, dog, cat, deer, seal, kangaroo, cow, bull, goat, monkey, hare, many other animals. "Highly recommended," DESIGN. Second, revised, enlarged edition with new plates from Cuvier, Stubbs, etc. 288 illustrations. 153pp. 11⅜ x 9.      T82 Clothbound $6.00

*ANIMAL DRAWING: ANATOMY AND ACTION FOR ARTISTS, C. R. Knight.* 158 studies, with full accompanying text, of such animals as the gorilla, bear, bison, dromedary, camel, vulture, pelican, iguana, shark, etc., by one of the greatest modern masters of animal drawing. Innumerable tips on how to get life expression into your work. "An excellent reference work," SAN FRANCISCO CHRONICLE. 158 illustrations. 156pp. 10½ x 8½.      T426 Paperbound $2.00

*PRINCIPLES OF ART HISTORY, H. Wölfflin.* This remarkably instructive work demonstrates the tremendous change in artistic conception from the 14th to the 18th centuries, by analyzing 164 works by Botticelli, Dürer, Hobbema, Holbein, Hals, Titian, Rembrandt, Vermeer, etc., and pointing out exactly what is meant by "baroque," "classic," "primitive," "picturesque," and other basic terms of art history and criticism. "A remarkable lesson in the art of seeing," SAT. REV. OF LITERATURE. Translated from the 7th German edition. 150 illus. 254pp. 6⅛ x 9¼.      T276 Paperbound $2.00

*FOUNDATIONS OF MODERN ART, A. Ozenfant.* Stimulating discussion of human creativity from paleolithic cave painting to modern painting, architecture, decorative arts. Fully illustrated with works of Gris, Lipchitz, Léger, Picasso, primitive, modern artifacts, architecture, industrial art, much more. 226 illustrations. 368pp. 6⅛ x 9¼.      T215 Paperbound $2.00

*SHAKER FURNITURE, E. D. and F. Andrews.* The most illuminating study of Shaker furniture ever written. Covers chronology, craftsmanship, houses, shops, etc. Includes over 200 photographs of chairs, tables, clocks, beds, benches, etc. "Mr. & Mrs. Andrews know all there is to know about Shaker furniture," Mark Van Doren, NATION. 48 full-page plates. 192pp. 7⅞ x 10¾.      T679 Paperbound $2.00

*PRIMITIVE ART, Franz Boas.* A great American anthropologist covers theory, technical virtuosity, styles, symbolism, patterns, etc. of primitive art. The more than 900 illustrations will interest artists, designers, craftworkers. Over 900 illustrations. 376pp. 5⅜ x 8.      T25 Paperbound $2.00

*ON THE LAWS OF JAPANESE PAINTING, H. Bowie.* The best possible substitute for lessons from an Oriental master. Treats both spirit and technique; exercises for control of the brush; inks, brushes, colors; use of dots, lines to express whole moods, etc. 66 illus. 272 pp. 6⅛ x 9¼.      T30 Paperbound $1.95

*DESIGN FOR ARTISTS AND CRAFTSMEN, L. Wolchonok.* The most thorough course on the creation of art motifs and designs. Shows you step-by-step, with hundreds of examples and 113 detailed exercises, how to create original designs from geometric patterns, plants, birds, animals, humans, and man-made objects. "A great contribution to the field of design and crafts," N. Y. SOCIETY OF CRAFTSMEN. More than 1300 entirely new illustrations. xv + 207pp. 7⅞ x 10¾.
T274 Clothbound $4.95

*VITRUVIUS: TEN BOOKS ON ARCHITECTURE.* The most influential book in the history of architecture. 1st century A.D. Roman classic has influenced such men as Bramante, Palladio, Michelangelo, up to present. Classic principles of design, harmony, etc. Fascinating reading. Definitive English translation by Professor H. Morgan, Harvard. 344pp. 5⅜ x 8.
T645 Paperbound $2.00

*HAWTHORNE ON PAINTING.* Vivid re-creation, from students' notes, of instructions by Charles Hawthorne at Cape Cod School of Art. Essays, epigrammatic comments on color, form, seeing, techniques, etc. "Excellent," Time. 91pp. 5⅜ x 8.
T653 Paperbound $1.00

*THE HANDBOOK OF PLANT AND FLORAL ORNAMENT, R. G. Hatton.* 1200 line illustrations, from medieval, Renaissance herbals, of flowering or fruiting plants: garden flowers, wild flowers, medicinal plants, poisons, industrial plants, etc. A unique compilation that probably could not be matched in any library in the world. Formerly "The Craftsman's Plant-Book." Also full text on uses, history as ornament, etc. 548pp. 6⅛ x 9¼.
T649 Paperbound $2.98

*DECORATIVE ALPHABETS AND INITIALS, Alexander Nesbitt.* 91 complete alphabets, over 3900 ornamental initials, from Middle Ages, Renaissance printing, baroque, rococo, and modern sources. Individual items copyright free, for use in commercial art, crafts, design, packaging, etc. 123 full-page plates. 3924 initials. 129pp. 7¾ x 10¾.
T544 Paperbound $2.25

*METHODS AND MATERIALS OF THE GREAT SCHOOLS AND MASTERS, Sir Charles Eastlake.* (Formerly titled "Materials for a History of Oil Painting.") Vast, authentic reconstruction of secret techniques of the masters, recreated from ancient manuscripts, contemporary accounts, analysis of paintings, etc. Oils, fresco, tempera, varnishes, encaustics. Both Flemish and Italian schools, also British and French. One of great works for art historians, critics; inexhaustible mine of suggestions, information for practicing artists. Total of 1025pp. 5⅜ x 8.
Two volume set, T718-9 Paperbound $4.00

*THE CRAFTSMAN'S HANDBOOK, Cennino Cennini.* The finest English translation of IL LIBRO DELL' ARTE, the 15th century introduction to art technique that is both a mirror of Quattrocento life and a source of many useful but nearly forgotten facets of the painter's art. 4 illustrations. xxvii + 142pp. D. V. Thompson, translator. 5⅜ x 8.
T54 Paperbound $1.35

*AFRICAN SCULPTURE, Ladislas Segy.* 163 full-page plates illustrating masks, fertility figures, ceremonial objects, etc., of 50 West and Central African tribes—95% never before illustrated. 34-page introduction to African sculpture. "Mr. Segy is one of its top authorities," NEW YORKER. 164 full-page photographic plates. Introduction. Bibliography. 244pp. 6⅛ x 9¼.
T396 Paperbound $2.00

*CALLIGRAPHY, J. G. Schwandner.* First reprinting in 200 years of this legendary book of beautiful handwriting. Over 300 ornamental initials, 12 complete calligraphic alphabets, over 150 ornate frames and panels, 75 calligraphic pictures of cherubs, stags, lions, etc., thousands of flourishes, scrolls, etc., by the greatest 18th-century masters. All material can be copied or adapted without permission. Historical introduction. 158 full-page plates. 368pp. 9 x 13.
T475 Clothbound $10.00

*A DIDEROT PICTORIAL ENCYCLOPEDIA OF TRADES AND INDUSTRY.* Manufacturing and the Technical Arts in Plates Selected from "L'Encyclopédie ou Dictionnaire Raisonné des Sciences, des Arts, et des Métiers," of Denis Diderot, edited with text by C. Gillispie. Over 2000 illustrations on 485 full-page plates. Magnificent 18th-century engravings of men, women, and children working at such trades as milling flour, cheesemaking, charcoal burning, mining, silverplating, shoeing horses, making fine glass, printing, hundreds more, showing details of machinery, different steps in sequence, etc. A remarkable art work, but also the largest collection of working figures in print, copyright-free, for art directors, designers, etc. Two vols. 920pp. 9 x 12. Heavy library cloth.
T421 Two volume set $18.50

*SILK SCREEN TECHNIQUES, J. Biegeleisen, M. Cohn.* A practical step-by-step home course in one of the most versatile, least expensive graphic arts processes. How to build an inexpensive silk screen, prepare stencils, print, achieve special textures, use color, etc. Every step explained, diagrammed. 149 illustrations, 8 in color. 201pp. 6⅛ x 9¼.
T433 Paperbound $1.55

*METALWORK AND ENAMELLING, H. Maryon.* Probably the best book ever written on the subject. Tells everything necessary for the home manufacture of jewelry, rings, ear pendants, bowls, etc. Covers materials, tools, soldering, filigree, setting stones, raising patterns, repoussé work, damascening, niello, cloisonné, polishing, assaying, casting, and dozens of other techniques. The best substitute for apprenticeship to a master metalworker. 363 photos and figures. 374pp. 5½ x 8½.
T183 Clothbound $8.50

*THE BROWN DECADES, Lewis Mumford.* A picture of the "buried renaissance" of the post-Civil War period, and the founding of modern architecture (Sullivan, Richardson, Root, Roebling), landscape development (Marsh, Olmstead, Eliot), and the graphic arts (Homer, Eakins, Ryder). 2nd revised, enlarged edition. Bibliography. 12 illustrations. xiv + 266 pp. 5⅜ x 8.
T200 Paperbound $1.65

*THE HUMAN FIGURE, J. H. Vanderpoel.* Not just a picture book, but a complete course by a famous figure artist. Extensive text, illustrated by 430 pencil and charcoal drawings of both male and female anatomy. 2nd enlarged edition. Foreword. 430 illus. 143pp. 6⅛ x 9¼.
T432 Paperbound $1.50

*PINE FURNITURE OF EARLY NEW ENGLAND, R. H. Kettell.* Over 400 illustrations, over 50 working drawings of early New England chairs, benches, beds, cupboards, mirrors, shelves, tables, other furniture esteemed for simple beauty and character. "Rich store of illustrations . . . emphasizes the individuality and varied design," ANTIQUES. 413 illustrations, 55 working drawings. 475pp. 8 x 10¾.
T145 Clothbound $10.00

*BASIC BOOKBINDING, A. W. Lewis.* Enables both beginners and experts to rebind old books or bind paperbacks in hard covers. Treats materials, tools; gives step-by-step instruction in how to collate a book, sew it, back it, make boards, etc. 261 illus. Appendices. 155pp. 5⅜ x 8.
T169 Paperbound $1.45

*THE BOOK OF SIGNS, R. Koch.* 493 symbols—crosses, monograms, astrological, biological symbols, runes, etc.—from ancient manuscripts, cathedrals, coins, catacombs, pottery. May be reproduced permission-free. 493 illustrations by Fritz Kredel. 104pp. 6⅛ x 9¼.
T162 Paperbound $1.00

*A HANDBOOK OF EARLY ADVERTISING ART, C. P. Hornung.* The largest collection of copyright-free early advertising art ever compiled. Vol. I: 2,000 illustrations of animals, old automobiles, buildings, allegorical figures, fire engines, Indians, ships, trains, more than 33 other categories! Vol. II: Over 4,000 typographical specimens; 600 Roman, Gothic, Barnum, Old English faces; 630 ornamental type faces; hundreds of scrolls, initials, flourishes, etc. "A remarkable collection," PRINTERS' INK.
Vol. I: Pictorial Volume. Over 2000 illustrations. 256pp. 9 x 12.
T122 Clothbound $10.00
Vol. II: Typographical Volume. Over 4000 specimens. 319pp. 9 x 12.
T123 Clothbound $10.00
Two volume set, Clothbound, only $18.50

*THE HISTORY AND TECHNIQUE OF LETTERING, A. Nesbitt.* A thorough history of lettering from the ancient Egyptians to the present, and a 65-page course in lettering for artists. Every major development in lettering history is illustrated by a complete alphabet. Fully analyzes such masters as Caslon, Koch, Garamont, Jenson, and many more. 89 alphabets, 165 other specimens. 317pp. 7½ x 10½.
T427 Paperbound $2.00

*LETTERING AND ALPHABETS, J. A. Cavanagh.* An unabridged reissue of "Lettering," containing the full discussion, analysis, illustration of 89 basic hand lettering styles based on Caslon, Bodoni, Gothic, many other types. Hundreds of technical hints on construction, strokes, pens, brushes, etc. 89 alphabets, 72 lettered specimens, which may be reproduced permission-free. 121pp. 9¾ x 8.
T53 Paperbound $1.25

*THE HUMAN FIGURE IN MOTION, Eadweard Muybridge.* The largest collection in print of Muybridge's famous high-speed action photos. 4789 photographs in more than 500 action-strip-sequences (at shutter speeds up to 1/6000th of a second) illustrate men, women, children—mostly undraped—performing such actions as walking, running, getting up, lying down, carrying objects, throwing, etc. "An unparalleled dictionary of action for all artists," AMERICAN ARTIST. 390 full-page plates, with 4789 photographs. Heavy glossy stock, reinforced binding with headbands. 7⅞ x 10¾.
T204 Clothbound $10.00

*ANIMALS IN MOTION, Eadweard Muybridge.* The largest collection of animal action photos in print. 34 different animals (horses, mules, oxen, goats, camels, pigs, cats, lions, gnus, deer, monkeys, eagles—and 22 others) in 132 characteristic actions. All 3919 photographs are taken in series at speeds up to 1/1600th of a second, offering artists, biologists, cartoonists a remarkable opportunity to see exactly how an ostrich's head bobs when running, how a lion puts his foot down, how an elephant's knee bends, how a bird flaps his wings, thousands of other hard-to-catch details. "A really marvellous series of plates," NATURE. 380 full-page plates. Heavy glossy stock; reinforced binding with headbands. 7⅞ x 10¾.
T203 Clothbound $10.00

*Dover publishes books on commercial art, art history, crafts, design, art classics; also books on music, literature, science, mathematics, puzzles and entertainments, chess, engineering, biology, philosophy, psychology, languages, history, and other fields. For free circulars write to Dept. DA, Dover Publications, Inc., 180 Varick St., New York 14, N.Y.*